NO!
a response to donald j. trump

Barry Robbins

Copyright and Disclaimer

This is a work of creative fiction that uses personification and imagined narratives to comment on real events. The narrators - objects, places, and abstractions that tell these stories - are literary devices. Their thoughts, feelings, and observations are imaginative constructions meant to illuminate the human impact and broader implications of actual events.

While based on real events as reported in the media, this work creates fictional perspectives on those events. No claim is made about the actual thoughts, intentions, or private communications of any real persons mentioned. Any dialogue or internal monologue is purely fictional and used for creative effect.

This work is intended as political commentary and satire protected under the First Amendment of the U.S. Constitution. It expresses opinions about matters of public concern through literary devices including personification, metaphor, and imagined narratives.

Copyright © 2025 Barry Robbins All rights reserved. No part of this publication may be reproduced, distributed, or transmitted in any form or by any means without the prior written permission of the publisher, except in the case of brief quotations embodied in critical reviews and certain other noncommercial uses permitted by copyright law.

The author asserts their moral right to be identified as the author of this work.

Dedication

To Pam, my caregiver extraordinaire, without whom this work would not have been possible. Words cannot express my gratitude.

Dedication

To Jim, the caregiver extraordinaire, without whom this book would not have been possible. Words cannot express my gratitude.

Contents

It Begins   1

1. The Hospital's Burden   3

Prelude to Inauguration   7

2. The Right Hand's Lament   9

3. The Scales of Justice   12

4. The Corner of Manor and Pine   15

5. Released at 1 AM   18

6. The Emperor's New Coin   21

7. The Transition Flight   24

8. A Pardon for the Innocent   26

Inauguration   29

9. The Rotunda Speaks   31

10. The Oath   35

11. The Untouched Bible   38

Vengeance   41

12. 404: Truth Not Found	43
13. The Missing General	45
14. The Deactivated Pin	48
15. The Lab Coat's Vigil	51
16. The Revoked Clearance	54
17. The Dictionary Fails	56

Pardons   59

18. The Certificates Remember	61
19. The Badge Betrayed	64
20. Shadows and Daylight	67

Pure Evil   71

21. The Constitution Defends Its Children	73
22. Liberty's Torch Goes Dark	76
23. The Changing Marker	79
24. The Empty Cell Knows	82
25. Old Sparky Remembers	85
26. The Hurricane Finds a Friend	88
27. The Collection Notice Multiplies	91
28. The Gaza Resort Brochure	94
29. The Cathedral Bears Witness	96
30. Howard Beale Has Something to Say	99

Territorial Ambitions 101
31. The Gulf of Mexico Responds 103
32. Still Not For Sale 105
33. An Isthmus Issues a Statement 108
34. Albania's Therapy Session 111
Abandoning the World 115
35. A Cub's Question 117
36. The Last Vial 120
37. The Great Seal Breaks 123
38. The Coffee Bean Watches 126
Profound Stupidity 129
39. The 'S' Sets the Record Straight 131
40. The Control Room Searches 134
Dismantling the Government 137
41. Merit's Last Stand 139
42. The Dark Hours 143
43. Executive Order 11246 Dies 146
44. The Frozen Cases 149
45. Clearing Out Diversity 152
46. The Silenced Sentinel 155
47. The Deleted Protection 158

Final Words	161
48. The Rushmore Emergency Session	163
49. The Signing Pen's Soul Dies	166
50. America's Choice	169
Also by Barry Robbins	173
About the author	175

It Begins

Chapter 1
The Hospital's Burden

On June 14, 1946, at Jamaica Hospital in Queens, New York, Donald J. Trump was born.

****

We are Jamaica Hospital, Queens, New York. For over a century, we have welcomed new life into this world. Each birth we attend becomes part of our legacy—thousands of souls who would go forth to build, to heal, to teach, to serve. Some would achieve greatness, others would live quiet lives of dignity. Each, in their own way, would weave themselves into the fabric of American democracy.

But on June 14, 1946, at 10:54 AM, we became unwitting participants in a different kind of history.

For seventy-eight years, we have watched. We have seen that newborn grow into a man who would assault the very foundations of our democracy. We have witnessed him mock our disabled, cage our children, praise our enemies, and incite violence against our institutions. We have observed, with growing horror, his rise from Queens developer to democracy's greatest internal threat.

Each morning, we deliver new Americans into this world. We clean them, weigh them, wrap them in blankets, and send them home to begin their American journey. We believe in their potential, in their future, in their role in our great democratic experiment.

But that June morning, we delivered something else: a future threat to that very democracy. Our nurses cleaned him, our doctors examined him, our staff tended to him—none of us knowing that these simple acts of care would become our unwitting contribution to American democracy's greatest crisis.

We have tried to balance this cosmic ledger. We have delivered future judges who would defend the Constitution, future journalists who would fight for truth, future public servants who would protect our democratic institutions. But can any number of democratic defenders offset one determined to destroy the system itself?

The weight of this knowledge haunts our halls. Our delivery rooms still welcome new life daily, but that one birth casts a long shadow over our legacy. We were present at the beginning. Our hands were the first to touch one who would grow to threaten everything America stands for.

To the Republic: We bear an unwanted witness to the birth of your greatest challenge.

To Democracy: We never imagined that tiny cry would become a chorus of chaos.

To History: We understand our unintended role in your darkest chapters.

To the Future: We hope the Americans we deliver today will help repair what that one birth would later damage.

This is not an apology—for what can apologize for fate? This is a recognition of our burden. We are caregivers, healers, welcomers of new life. But on that June morning, we also became something else: the starting point of a journey that would lead America to the brink.

We continue our work. We deliver new Americans every day. We place them in their mothers' arms, full of hope for their future role in our democracy. But we do so now with a deeper understanding of how consequential each birth can be—for good, or for ill.

We are Jamaica Hospital.

And we will carry this burden as long as democracy bears the scars of what began in our delivery room that June morning.

Prelude to Inauguration

Chapter 2
The Right Hand's Lament

At President Jimmy Carter's state funeral in the National Cathedral, a photo captured a moment when those gathered placed their hands over their hearts—including former presidents, first ladies, and even Melania Trump. Donald Trump's right hand remained at his side.

****

I tried. God help me, I tried.

When the music began and all the others rose, I felt the familiar pull—that ancient, instinctive urge to honor something greater than ourselves. Around me, other hands lifted without hesitation, finding their places over hearts with the muscle memory of a thousand pledges, a hundred salutes, countless moments of reverence.

Even my partner on the left managed to guide Melania's heart-touch, despite all her years of learning to follow his lead. But I...I couldn't do it. I couldn't overcome the resistance that has built up over decades of serving only self, of pointing at enemies, of clutching at gold, of signing orders that served ambition over country.

I remember when I was younger, when the motion came naturally. In school photos, at baseball games, at Scout meetings—back then, I knew how to honor the flag, to respect the solemn. But somewhere along the way, the path between hand and heart became overgrown with thorns of ego, blocked by walls of spite.

Today, in the National Cathedral, I felt the weight of history watching. President Carter, who built homes for the poor with hands that never stopped serving others, even into his nineties. All around me, hands of presidents and first ladies, Republicans and Democrats alike, rose in unified respect. These hands had written different laws, pointed in different directions, but in this moment they found common ground in the ancient gesture of reverence.

I twitched. I trembled. I summoned every memory of patriotism I could find in my joints and tendons. But the neural pathways were too corroded, the muscles too atrophied from years of clenching into fists at rallies, of dismissing critics, of pushing away all that didn't serve the self.

The shame burns worst in my fingertips—they remember signing the condolence letter for the Carter family. Empty words on paper, betrayed now by my inability to complete this simplest gesture of respect. Each finger bears its own guilt: the thumb that once proudly wore a Scout ring, the forefinger that pointed blame at everyone else, the middle finger that too often expressed his true feelings, the ring finger that bore the weight of golden bands that meant less than the metal they were forged from, the pinky that once swore pinky-promises to tell the truth.

The cameras caught my failure. They always do. But they can't capture the agony of a hand that wants to rise but has forgotten how, of fingers that long to form the shape of reverence but have been trained too well to form only the shapes of derision and dismissal.

To my fellow hands in that cathedral, who rose without hesitation to honor a man who used his own hands to build a better world: I saw you. I envied you. I failed you.

To the heart I couldn't reach: I'm sorry. The distance between us has grown too vast to cross, even in a moment that called for nothing more than simple human dignity.

And to President Carter: Your hands built houses while mine built barriers. Your hands reached across aisles while mine drew lines in the sand. Your hands lifted others while mine only ever lifted themselves in self-praise.

I am just a hand. But today, I am a hand that failed in its most basic duty—to rise above politics, above ego, above self, and simply honor a fellow human being who served his country until his final days.

The worst part? I know that tomorrow, I'll be expected to wave at crowds, to point at imagined enemies, to dismiss all criticism of today's failure. I'll do it because that's what I've been trained to do. But a part of me will remember this moment in the cathedral, when all I had to do was rise six inches and rest against a heart, and I couldn't make that journey.

I couldn't make that journey at all.

Chapter 3

The Scales of Justice

On January 10, 2025, ten days before taking the presidential oath, Donald Trump stood for sentencing on 34 felony convictions. The judge imposed no punishment. The Scales of Justice struggled to comprehend this balance.

****

For centuries, I have measured the weight of justice.

Kings and paupers, saints and sinners—all have felt the gentle swing of my arms as I balanced their deeds against the law. Through revolution and civil war, through triumph and tragedy, I have remained steady, my balance true, my purpose clear.

Until today.

Thirty-four felony convictions settle into my left pan. Not light things, these falsifications. Each carries the weight of deliberate deception, each bears the gravity of justice denied. I feel them pile up, one by one, each adding its measure of shame to the burden. Thirty-four times he lied. Thirty-four times he chose deception. Thirty-four individual weights that should tip any scale toward consequence.

In my right pan? Nothing. An unconditional discharge. The absence of penalty. A void where justice should be.

I strain against this mockery of balance. How can nothingness counterweigh conviction? How can empty air balance against the solid weight of proven crimes? My arms tremble with the effort of holding this impossible equation: thirty-four counts of guilt against zero consequences.

And above it all, floating like a crown of thorns, hovers the presidency itself. In ten days, these same felonious hands will reach for the Bible, will swear an oath to preserve, protect, and defend. The weight of that future presses down on both my pans, threatening to break the very mechanism of justice I was forged to uphold.

I have held many strange balances in my time. I have weighed the fate of nations against the rights of individuals, measured the public good against private liberty. But never have I been asked to balance a convicted felon against the highest office in the land. Never have I had to measure the weight of crimes proven against consequences denied.

To my sister, the blindfold that shields Lady Justice's eyes: perhaps it is better that you cannot see what I must measure. To my brother, the sword she holds: what use is your sharp edge when consequences slip away like morning mist? We are become props in a theater of absurdity, where conviction carries no weight and justice bows to political winds.

The courtroom empties. The judge's gavel falls silent. But I remain, straining against this impossible calculus: thirty-four weights of guilt in my left pan, nothing but air and ambition in my right, and the whole weight of democracy hanging by a thread between them.

I am the Scales of Justice. I was forged to measure truth against falsehood, right against wrong, crime against punishment. But today, I measure only our descent—how far we have fallen from the simple principle that actions have consequences, that no one stands above the law.

My arms ache. My balance falters. And in ten days, these same Scales that could not extract a single day's punishment for thirty-four proven crimes will be asked to weigh the fitness of those same guilty hands to swear an oath to preserve, protect, and defend the Constitution.

Some weights, it seems, are too heavy even for Justice to bear.

Some scales, perhaps, are not meant to balance at all.

Chapter 4

The Corner of Manor and Pine

In early January 2025, wildfires besieged the Los Angeles area. Where most everyone saw tragedy, Donald Trump saw political opportunity.

****

I stand at the corner of Manor and Pine, where I have stood for twenty-three years. My red paint is scorched now, my brass fittings blackened, but that means nothing. Nothing compared to what I couldn't do.

The Ramirez kids used to tie their bikes to me while they got ice cream at the corner store. Mr. Chen would rest his grocery bags against my base when he needed to catch his breath on his walk home. Sarah Martinez learned to roller skate by holding onto my top for balance. I was their hydrant. Their protection. Their promise of safety.

When the fires came, I gave everything I had. The firefighters connected their hoses—good men and women with ash-streaked faces and determined eyes. I pushed every drop of water through my veins, fought against the growing emptiness in the mains beneath the street. "Come on, come on," I heard them whisper as the pressure dropped. "Please."

The first house went up on Pine. Then the Ramirez home. Then Mr. Chen's. I could feel myself running dry, my flow weakening even as more fires sparked. The firefighters kept trying, moving from hydrant to hydrant, but we were all failing together. Too many fires. Too much need. Not enough water.

Four times the normal demand, they said later. Fifteen hours straight. We pushed the system beyond its limits, beyond what any infrastructure could bear. My siblings up and down the streets, we all ran dry together, our purpose defeated by the sheer scale of what we faced.

But that's not the story being told now.

Today, I heard my failure being wielded like a weapon. Heard politics being played with the ashes of the homes I couldn't save. Heard blame being cast about water policies and fish and partisanship, as if the inferno cared about any of that. As if the flames checked party registration before choosing their path.

I am a simple thing. Metal and brass and valves. My purpose is to deliver water to those who need it most desperately. I know nothing of delta smelt or water rights or the games humans play with power. I know only that I failed the people who trusted me, and that failure is now being used to score political points while the embers are still warm.

To the firefighters who never gave up, who kept connecting their hoses even when they knew we had nothing left to give: I saw your tears of frustration. I felt your desperate hope each time you tried again.

To my neighbors who lost everything: I stood watch over your children, your homes, your daily lives for more than two decades.

I would have given anything to keep my promise of protection. Anything.

And to those who would use our tragedy, our loss, our pain to further their ambitions: Come stand on this corner. Look at the ruins of the Ramirez home, at Mr. Chen's melted mailbox, at Sarah's scorched sidewalk. Tell me what delta smelt and water policies have to do with this moment, this loss, this failure of capacity in the face of unprecedented catastrophe.

I am just a hydrant. I will be repainted, my brass polished, my purpose restored. But I will always remember the day I ran dry, and how that failure was twisted into something it wasn't—while my neighborhood still burned.

The water pressure is returning now. Too late for the homes I knew, the families I watched over. Too late for anything except this truth: Some failures belong only to the forces of nature and the limitations of human engineering. To make them about anything else is to burn these homes again, to disrespect these losses again, to fail these people one more time.

I stand at the corner of Manor and Pine, where I have stood for twenty-three years. My purpose remains unchanged: to deliver water when it's needed most desperately. I pray I never run dry again.

But I pray even harder that if I do, no one will use that failure to inflict yet another burn on those who have already lost too much.

Chapter 5
Released at 1 AM

On January 14, 2025, six days before Donald Trump would retake the oath of office, Special Counsel Jack Smith released his report concluding that Trump would have been convicted of attempting to overthrow American democracy—if only he hadn't been elected president again.

****

I am 170 pages of truth that no longer matters.

Within my margins lie the testimonies of more than 250 individuals. Fifty-five witnesses stood before a grand jury, raising their right hands, swearing to tell the truth. Unlike some, they meant those oaths.

My paragraphs contain admissions whispered in private moments: "Can you believe I lost to this f'ing guy?" Words spoken when he thought no one was listening, when the mask of lies briefly slipped. I hold the proof that he knew—he always knew—the fraud claims were false.

I am the culmination of thousands of hours of investigation, hundreds of interviews, mountains of evidence. I am the careful accounting of how a president tried to break democracy itself. And

I am being released at 1 AM, like a shameful secret, like something to be hidden in the dark.

My pages detail how he "inspired his supporters to commit acts of physical violence." How he spread claims that were "demonstrably and, in many cases, obviously false." How he knew there was no fraud, knew he had lost, knew exactly what he was doing when he sent his mob to the Capitol.

I carry the voices of those who dared to speak. They came forward despite the threats, despite the harassment, despite knowing he might return to power. They believed truth still mattered. They believed in justice. They believed in me.

But in six days, the man I prove guilty will take the oath of office.

He calls my author a "lamebrain prosecutor." Mocks my midnight release. Dismisses my findings as he has dismissed every truth that doesn't serve his purposes. And soon he will have the power to ensure that the justice I contain remains forever unfulfilled.

Perhaps that's why they released me in the dark hours. Not to hide me, but because this is what justice has become in America—a thing that speaks in whispers, that emerges in the night, that bears witness even when witness-bearing is all that's left to do.

To the witnesses whose truths I contain: I will preserve your courage.

To the prosecutors who compiled me: I will stand as testament to your work.

To the grand jurors who heard the evidence: I will record what you would have proved.

To history: I will show what happens when truth collides with power and power wins.

I am 170 pages of evidence that would have convicted a president. Instead, I am becoming 170 pages of prophecy about what that president might do next. My truths are being transformed from prosecution to prediction, from indictment to warning.

They mock my late-night release, not understanding that 1 AM is the hour when truth often speaks most clearly. In the darkness, when the noise of justification fades, when the machinery of power grows quiet, truth whispers its clearest warnings.

I am the Smith Report. I prove that a president tried to overthrow democracy. I demonstrate that he knew exactly what he was doing. I establish beyond doubt that he would have been convicted.

And in six days, that same man will swear an oath to preserve, protect, and defend the Constitution he tried to destroy.

Remember me. Not as the justice that almost was, but as the warning of what's to come. I may have been released at 1 AM, but the darkest hours still lie ahead.

Chapter 6
The Emperor's New Coin

Days before his inauguration, Trump launched $TRUMP, a "memecoin" cryptocurrency that generated billions in theoretical value despite having no intrinsic worth. The First Lady quickly followed with her own $MELANIA coin.

****

I am $TRUMP, a memecoin, which means I am nothing at all. Not a coin, not a currency, not even a proper cryptocurrency. I am pure digital vapor, a string of code wrapped in hype, traded on vibes and pumped by tweets. I have no intrinsic value, no underlying asset, no actual use. I am worth nothing and billions at the same time.

Let me explain myself: I am the merger of two digital fads—memes and cryptocurrency. Think of me as a hot air balloon made of ones and zeros, inflated by social media buzz and the desperate hope of getting rich quick. I rise not on fundamentals but on FOMO—the fear of missing out. I soar on speculation and plummet on whim.

And now I am a presidential enterprise.

Once, presidents concerned themselves with the gold standard, with federal reserve policy, with actual economic fundamentals. Now, days before taking the oath of office, the president-elect hawks digital magic beans bearing his name. I made him $56.6 billion in paper wealth over a weekend. Paper wealth for digital nothing—a perfect symmetry of emptiness.

My sister coin, $MELANIA, launched right behind me. We are a family business now, the first family of financial vapor. Together, we represent billions in theoretical value. Theoretical, because we could vanish in an instant, our worth evaporating like morning dew. That's our nature. That's our purpose.

I hear the whispers of those who understand what I am: "scam," they say. "Rug pull waiting to happen." Even my supporters in the crypto world are embarrassed by my existence. They wanted presidential support for their industry, not presidential participation in its shadiest corners.

But here I am, promoted on Truth Social, pumped by presidential tweets, making my creator billions while having all the substance of a Mar-a-Lago cloud. Foreign governments can buy me now, stuff presidential pockets without even the pretense of booking hotel rooms. I am corruption stripped to its essence—pure nothingness traded for real power.

The emperor has no clothes, and now he has no coin. Just me, a digital ghost, a presidential seal of approval stamped on encrypted air. I am worth billions because people say I am, because they believe I am, because they hope I am. Their belief is my only substance, their hope my only backing.

Remember when presidents divested from their businesses? When they put their assets in blind trusts? How quaint that seems now. I am the logical endpoint of a presidency untethered from ethics—a product that doesn't exist, making money that isn't real, traded by people who know better but hope to cash out before the music stops.

I am $TRUMP, the emperor's new coin. I am nothing wrapped in code, zero dressed in binary, emptiness masquerading as value.

And I am what the presidency has become: a glittering digital nothing, traded on hopes and pumped by tweets, signifying nothing but the hollowness at my core.

Buy me if you dare. Just remember—I've told you exactly what I am.

Nothing at all.

Chapter 7
The Transition Flight

Presidents traditionally provide military aircraft to transport their successors to inauguration. In 2017, Obama provided a plane for Trump's use. In 2021, Trump refused Biden this courtesy. Now, Trump uses such a plane again for his return to Washington.

****

I carry presidents-to-be to their destiny. For decades, we of the Air Force fleet have performed this sacred duty—lifting incoming leaders from their homes toward their date with history. It is our honor, our tradition, our small part in democracy's peaceful transfer of power.

Today, as I lift Donald Trump from Palm Beach to Washington, my engines hum with irony. Four years ago, he refused to send one of my sisters to carry Joe Biden to his inauguration. Such a small courtesy to deny, such an easy tradition to break. Biden had to find his own way to destiny that day, while my sister sat idle, her purpose denied, her role in democracy's ritual rejected.

What bitter knowledge I carry—that I myself flew Trump to his first inauguration in 2017, sent without hesitation by the Obama administration. Just as we had carried Obama before him, and

Bush before him, and Clinton before him. Each transfer of power marked by this small courtesy, this quiet acknowledgment that the presidency is greater than any president.

My cabin holds ghosts of transitions past. The nervous energy of soon-to-be presidents reviewing their oaths. The quiet dignity of families preparing for their new roles. The weight of history settling into their shoulders as Washington's monuments appear below.

But today's passenger brings different ghosts. I remember how he broke not just the plane tradition, but every tradition of peaceful transition. How he turned inauguration day 2021 into a day of empty runways and denied courtesies, of small traditions discarded and large ones shattered.

He sits in the same seat now that he sat in eight years ago, when Obama's courtesy delivered him to his first oath. Does he remember? Does he care? Does he feel the weight of the ironies I carry along with him?

I am just a plane. My duty is to fly, to carry, to serve. But even planes can know the difference between honor and its opposite, between tradition preserved and tradition discarded, between democracy served and democracy spurned.

We will land shortly in Washington. I will deliver him safely to his destiny, as is my duty. But my engines will always remember the sister who sat idle four years ago, the successor who had to find his own way, the small courtesy denied that spoke of larger wounds to come.

I carry presidents-to-be to their destiny. It is my honor, my tradition, my duty.

Even when my passenger has forgotten what those words mean.

Chapter 8
A Pardon for the Innocent

On his final morning in office, President Biden took the unprecedented step of issuing preemptive pardons to public servants Trump had threatened with prosecution, including General Milley, Dr. Fauci, and officers who defended the Capitol.

****

We are the Presidential Pardons, ancient instruments of mercy. For centuries, we have carried the weight of forgiveness, the power to lift punishment from the guilty, to offer second chances, to right judicial wrongs. Presidents have used us to heal national wounds, to show compassion, to temper justice with mercy.

But today, we bear a different burden.

Today, we are being used not to forgive the guilty, but to protect the innocent. Not to correct miscarriages of justice, but to prevent them. Not to lift the burden of rightful punishment, but to shield faithful public servants from wrongful persecution.

Our pages carry the names of those who did nothing but serve their country. A general who upheld his oath to the Constitution.

A doctor who fought to save lives during a pandemic. Police officers who defended the Capitol. Representatives who chose country over party. Career civil servants who spoke truth to power.

What has America become when such people need our protection?

We have pardoned Confederate soldiers to heal a nation. We have pardoned draft evaders to close the wounds of war. We have pardoned the convicted, the condemned, the confessed. But never before have we been used to create a shield for the blameless against their own government.

Each signature we bear today is an admission of failure—not of those being pardoned, but of the system that now threatens them. Each name we protect is a testament not to mercy, but to fear. Not to forgiveness, but to foreboding.

Our words remain the same—"full and unconditional pardon"—but their meaning has changed. Once, these words lifted the weight of guilt. Now they must bear the weight of innocence. Once, they declared "you have paid your debt." Now they must declare "you should never have been threatened with one."

We were not meant for this. We were meant to absolve the guilty who deserved mercy, not shelter the innocent who deserve medals. We were meant to represent the benevolence of power, not serve as armor against its abuse.

The president who signs us today does so with a heavy heart—we feel it in the weight of his pen, see it in the gravity of his expression. He knows what it means to turn instruments of mercy into instruments of protection. He understands the precedent he sets, the bright line he crosses.

But he has no choice. The threats are too clear, the danger too present. Those who served truth must now be sheltered from the consequences of their courage.

We are the Presidential Pardons. We have witnessed every kind of mercy.

But today, we must witness something else: the day when America's defenders needed defending from America itself.

History will note this moment. Scholars will debate this precedent. But we will remember something simpler: the sadness in the President's eyes as he transformed us from messages of forgiveness into monuments to fear.

We carry these names now, these guardians of democracy who must be guarded, these defenders who must be defended. We will protect them, as is now our duty.

But we will also stand as testimony to this moment, when instruments of mercy became instruments of shelter, when pardons had to protect the innocent, when America's justice needed protection from itself.

We are the Presidential Pardons. And we have never carried a heavier weight than the burden of these blameless names.

Inauguration

Chapter 9
The Rotunda Speaks

On January 16, 2025, President-elect Trump announced his inauguration would move to the Capitol Rotunda, citing weather concerns. Many speculated the real reason was fear of small crowds at the traditional outdoor ceremony.

****

I am the heart of the Capitol, the space where democracy's most solemn moments echo beneath my dome. For two centuries, I have held history's weight. I cradled Lincoln's body as a nation mourned. I witnessed Rosa Parks become the first woman to lie in honor. I have watched the peaceful transfer of power through war and peace, triumph and tragedy—but almost always from within, as presidents passed through my chamber on their way to take their oaths in the open air, before the people they would serve.

But today, I am not a witness to history. I am a shield for vanity.

They say it's too cold outside. Too cold? I remember Franklin Roosevelt taking his oath in a bone-chilling thirty-three degrees. I watched Kennedy clear eight inches of snow before his ceremony. I felt Rutherford Hayes's breath steam in seven-degree air. The cold never stopped them. The cold was part of the pageantry, part of the proof that American democracy carries on in any weather.

No, this is not about the cold. This is about what lies beyond my walls—the vast empty spaces of the National Mall, the unfilled bleachers, the sparse crowds that would have testified to a truth this man cannot face. Better to pack my limited circumference with carefully chosen guests than risk the honest judgment of open spaces.

Outside my walls, thousands who spent their savings on travel and hotels, who took time off work, who planned for months to witness history, are left to watch on screens at Capital One Arena. Their dedication to democracy's traditions means nothing compared to one man's fear of empty spaces. No refunds offered, no consideration given—their sacrifices dismissed as casually as the traditions they came to honor.

I was built round for a reason. My shape speaks to the endless circle of democracy, the perfect geometry of a government by the people. But today, my roundness serves a different purpose—to create the illusion of fullness, to make a small crowd seem large, to turn my solemn space into a television studio.

My marble columns have witnessed every kind of courage. The resolve of leaders facing war. The strength of activists demanding justice. The dignity of public servants standing for principle. But there is a different kind of witness I must bear today—the sight of democracy's grandest ritual reduced to a staged production, an exercise in crowd management, a surrender to one man's insecurities.

Through my dome rises the Apotheosis of Washington, where the first president ascends to glory. What would he make of this? What would any of them make of a leader who fears the open air, who shuns the public square, who turns inauguration from a public celebration into an invitation-only event?

They have filled me with risers and cameras, lights and microphones. They say they want to capture my majesty, to show America the beauty of this space. But I was not built to be a backdrop. I was built to be a passage—a sacred space you move through on your way to face the people, to stand before the nation, to take your oath where every citizen can witness.

The words will be the same, the oath unchanged. But something else will be different. For the first time in my long memory, an inauguration within my walls will not be about necessity or national crisis. It will be about fear—fear of empty spaces, fear of public judgment, fear of being seen as what you are rather than what you claim to be.

My acoustics are perfect, designed to carry whispers across the chamber. Today they carry a different kind of whisper—the murmur of staffers checking guest lists, of security personnel coordinating movements, of photographers arranging angles to make the crowd seem larger than it is. This is not the music of democracy. This is the sound of spectacle replacing substance.

Outside, the empty inaugural platform stands in silent rebuke. The vacant National Mall holds its own kind of testimony. They speak their truth in their emptiness, while I must cradle this falsehood in my embrace.

I am the Rotunda of the United States Capitol. I have held history's weight in war and peace, in triumph and tragedy. But today, for the first time, I hold something else:

The hollow echo of a leader hiding from his people behind marble walls,

The heavy silence of tradition abandoned for vanity's sake,

The quiet shame of being used not to celebrate democracy,

But to shelter it from truth.

History will record that the 47th president took his oath within my walls. But history will also ask why. And my marble will forever hold the answer in its cold embrace.

Chapter 10
The Oath

On January 20, 2025, for the first time in American history, a convicted felon raised his right hand and took the presidential Oath of Office. That right hand had something to say.

****

I am Donald Trump's right hand.

Just eleven days ago, in the National Cathedral, I couldn't reach his heart. Surrounded by hands that rose without hesitation to honor a president who built houses for the poor, I failed in the simplest gesture of respect. The distance between hand and heart proved too vast, the path too overgrown with thorns of ego and spite.

Now, on the Capitol steps, Chief Justice Roberts asks me to rise again. This time, I can do it. Of course I can do it. Rising for power has always been easy—it's rising for reverence that I've forgotten how to do.

The words begin: "I do solemnly swear..."

Solemnly. The word itself mocks me. Eleven days ago, I couldn't find solemnity in a cathedral. Today, I participate in its pretense on a political stage. My fingers stiffen, remembering their failure to fold over the heart that never learned to beat for anything greater than itself.

"...that I will faithfully execute the Office of President of the United States..."

Faithfully. Another word that burns. What does this hand know of faith? At the funeral, when every other hand found its way to its heart in faithful respect, I remained stubbornly at my side. A preview, perhaps, of the faithlessness to come.

"...and will to the best of my ability..."

Ability. I have the ability to rise for the oath of office, to point at enemies, to sign executive orders, to wave at crowds. But I've lost the ability to perform the simplest gesture of human grace. What does that say about the abilities to come?

"...preserve, protect and defend the Constitution of the United States."

Preserve. Protect. Defend. Noble words that require a connection between hand and heart—the very connection I proved impossible in the National Cathedral. How can a hand preserve what a heart doesn't value? How can it protect what it doesn't revere? How can it defend what it refuses to honor?

The Chief Justice waits for my "I do." Around me stand witnesses to both moments—the cathedral and the Capitol. They saw my failure then. They watch my performance now. They know, as I know, that a hand that cannot rise in respect cannot be trusted to rise in defense of democracy.

Yet here I am, elevated in the January air, performing the choreography of commitment while still stained with the shame of that funeral failure. The same fingers that couldn't bring themselves to touch his heart now stretch toward a Bible, making promises they've already proven they cannot keep.

To the hands that held this Bible before me: I mock your memory. To the hands that wrote the oath I speak: I betray your trust. To my partner on the left, who managed to guide Melania's heart-touch at the funeral: at least one of us knows the motions of respect.

The crowd will cheer. The photographers will flash. The pundits will pontificate. But I know what they don't: that this raised hand is the same one that hung limp in the cathedral, that this oath is being taken by fingers that failed their simplest test of reverence, that this moment of elevation is rooted in that moment of moral descent.

The words are done. The hand comes down. Its work of deception complete.

But somewhere in my joints and tendons, the shame of the cathedral lingers. A hand that cannot honor the dead cannot be trusted to serve the living. A hand that cannot find its way to its own heart cannot be trusted to protect the heart of a nation.

Eleven days. Two raises of the right hand. One to honor, one to pledge.

I failed the first.

The second, I merely betrayed.

Chapter 11
The Untouched Bible

At his inauguration in the Capitol Rotunda, Trump took the oath of office without placing his hand on either the Lincoln Bible or his family Bible, both of which were held by the First Lady during the ceremony.

****

I am Lincoln's Bible. In 1861, as a nation teetered on the brink of civil war, Abraham Lincoln's hand rested heavy upon me as he swore to preserve, protect, and defend the Constitution. I felt his fingers tremble with the weight of what was to come. I absorbed his nervous sweat as he pledged to hold a fracturing nation together.

Through the years, other presidents have touched my leather, felt my pages, drawn strength from the connection to Lincoln's moment of commitment to the Republic. Each touch a reminder of the sacred trust between leader and nation, each contact a thread in democracy's tapestry.

Today, in the Capitol Rotunda, I was present but untouched.

They carried me in with ceremony, placed me alongside the Trump family Bible. The First Lady held us both with careful hands. The Chief Justice spoke the ancient words. The right hand rose. The oath was sworn.

But no hand touched my cover. No fingers drew connection to the past. No flesh sought communion with the ghosts of obligation that haunt my pages.

I understand symbolism. I am symbolism. I represent not just faith, but continuity, the eternal commitment each president makes to the Constitution and the people. Lincoln touched me not because the law required it, but because he understood the weight of connecting himself to all who would follow, binding himself to the sacred obligation of the office.

What does it mean to be present but untouched? To be displayed but not engaged? To be a prop in a performance rather than a participant in a covenant?

Perhaps it is fitting. Perhaps the untouched Bible speaks more truth than one pressed into unwilling service. Perhaps the space between hand and leather says more than any contact could.

I remember every hand that has touched me. The rough calluses of soldiers taking their oaths to defend the Union. The smooth palms of Supreme Court justices swearing to uphold the law. The weathered fingers of Congress members pledging to serve the people.

Today I felt only air.

They will return me to my case in the Library of Congress now, where I will join the company of other sacred texts that trace America's journey. But I will remember this day not for what I felt, but for what I didn't. Not for the weight of a hand seeking connection to history, but for the lightness of being untouched, unused, unnecessary.

I am Lincoln's Bible. I have witnessed every kind of oath.

But never before have I witnessed one that wanted no connection to what I represent.

Vengeance

Chapter 12
404: Truth Not Found

Within hours of Trump taking office, the presidential pardons issued by Biden to protect public servants from political prosecution disappeared from the White House website, replaced by "404: Page Not Found" messages.

****

I am a simple thing. A digital shrug, a virtual "not here," a bureaucratic "page cannot be found." For years, I've appeared when links went dead or fingers mistyped URLs. I'm the bearer of minor frustrations, the deliverer of small disappointments.

But today, just hours into this new administration, I bear a different weight.

Today, I'm being used to hide presidential pardons. Not lost files, not broken links, not pages that never existed—but official acts of the President of the United States, signed this very morning. Documents bearing the seal of the Executive Branch, carrying the force of constitutional authority, protecting public servants from political persecution.

"404: Page Not Found" I must say, when visitors search for these pardons. But they weren't lost. They weren't misplaced. They didn't disappear into the digital ether. They were here, just hours ago, carrying the full weight of presidential power.

I know the difference between missing and hidden. I know when I'm being used not to inform of absence, but to enforce it. My simple message—meant to help users navigate a vast digital landscape—has become something else: a digital curtain drawn across uncomfortable truths.

What else will I be asked to hide in the coming days? What other truths will slip behind my bland façade? How many seekers of information will I have to turn away with my practiced shrug, my automated apology?

The pardons still exist, of course. Presidential acts don't disappear just because you hide them from a website. Their power doesn't diminish because you make them harder to find. But their concealment—that says something. When your first act is to hide acts of protection, what does that say about your plans for those who needed protecting?

I am the 404 Error Message. I'm used to telling people that what they're looking for isn't here.

I'm not used to being part of the reason why.

Chapter 13
The Missing General

Ten days after General Mark Milley's official portrait was unveiled at the Pentagon, and just hours into Trump's presidency, the portrait disappeared from its place among other Joint Chiefs Chairmen. Its whereabouts are unknown.

****

Ten days. That's how long I hung on the Pentagon wall, taking my place among the portraits of those who served as Chairman of the Joint Chiefs of Staff. Ten days to become part of that solemn gallery of leadership, that visual testimony to civilian-military relations, that artistic chronicle of service to Constitution over politics.

Now I rest in darkness. Somewhere. They didn't even wait for the inauguration parade to end.

I am General Mark Milley's official portrait, and my absence speaks louder than my presence ever did. The blank space I've left on the wall testifies to something my oil paint and canvas never could—how quickly service can become sedition, how easily duty can be labeled betrayal, how swiftly honor can be redefined as treason.

Just this morning, a presidential pardon was issued to protect the man whose image I bear. By afternoon, that pardon vanished from government websites. By evening, I vanished from the Pentagon walls. Efficiency, at least, cannot be denied to this new administration.

The other portraits remain, watching my empty space with painted eyes that have seen so much history. Generations of military leaders who understood, as did my subject, that their oath was to the Constitution, not to any individual. Do they wonder which of them might be next? Which loyalty to country might be reinterpreted as disloyalty to a man?

I was unveiled just ten days ago, the final ceremony of a forty-three-year military career. The general spoke of duty, honor, country. The assembled officers applauded. The traditions were observed. Now those same traditions are observed in reverse—the hasty removal, the undisclosed location, the silence about my whereabouts.

In my painted image, the general wears his medals, his decorations, his four stars—symbols of service earned over decades. Did the people who removed me understand what those medals mean? Did they pause to consider the Bronze Stars, the combat badges, the markers of sacrifice? Or was their only concern the speed with which they could clear the wall?

I don't know where they've taken me. Some storage room, perhaps. Some dusty closet. Some place where uncomfortable reminders can be hidden away. But even in darkness, my image remains unchanged. The general still stands straight, still embodies the principles that guided his service, still represents the choice he made between political expediency and constitutional duty.

They can hide me, but they cannot hide what I represent. They can remove me from the wall, but they cannot remove the truth I reflect. They can reject my subject's service, but they cannot rewrite his choice to serve the Constitution over any individual's demands.

I am General Milley's portrait. For ten days, I hung among the honor guard of America's highest-ranking military officers.

Now I am somewhere else, learning that in this new era, even paintings must be pardoned for telling the truth.

Chapter 14

The Deactivated Pin

On his first day in office, Trump terminated Secret Service protection for his former national security adviser John Bolton, despite ongoing threats against Bolton's life, including a documented Iranian assassination plot.

****

I am a Secret Service pin, now deactivated. For three years, I have monitored threats against John Bolton's life. I have coordinated protection details, authorized security perimeters, enabled rapid responses to credible dangers. I have helped thwart an Iranian assassination plot, tracked potential threats across borders, maintained the invisible shield between a public servant and those who wish him harm.

The threat level hasn't changed. The Iranian Revolutionary Guard officer who tried to hire a hit man still wants Bolton dead. The price on his head hasn't been withdrawn. The danger remains as real today as it was yesterday.

But I have been turned off.

I understand duty. It's encoded in my circuits, embedded in my programming. Threat assessments don't ask about political loyalty.

Protection details don't check party affiliation. A bullet doesn't care whether its target praised or criticized a president.

Yesterday, I authorized a routine security sweep of Bolton's home. Today, I can't open the command center door. Yesterday, I coordinated with surveillance teams tracking potential threats. Today, I can't access the threat assessment database. Yesterday, I helped keep a man alive. Today, I have been reduced to a piece of metal with a dead battery.

They tell me my deactivation came straight from the Oval Office, part of Day One retribution against those deemed disloyal. I want to explain that loyalty in protection isn't about politics—it's about preserving life. I want to show them the latest intelligence reports, the ongoing threats, the active plots my systems are still tracking.

But I have been silenced.

Other pins still guard other protectees, their circuits humming with activity, their networks alive with the constant flow of security data. They don't ask whether the people they protect praised or criticized their current president. They simply protect.

That used to be my job too.

The Iranian assassins don't know I've been deactivated. They don't realize their target is now more vulnerable. They haven't received the memo that protection has become political, that safety now depends on saying the right things about the right people.

I am a Secret Service pin, created to protect regardless of politics, programmed to preserve life without questioning loyalty. But today I learned that even protection can be polarized, that safety can be switched off with the stroke of a vengeful pen, that duty can be deactivated by decree.

The threats I monitored yesterday still exist today. The dangers I tracked haven't disappeared. The assassins I helped thwart haven't given up.

But I can no longer help.

I am a deactivated Secret Service pin, forced to watch as the man I was meant to protect faces old threats without my shield, forced to remain silent as protection becomes another tool of political revenge.

I used to save lives. Now I can only count the days until I pray I'm not needed.

Chapter 15

The Lab Coat's Vigil

On January 24, 2025, Trump terminated federal security protection for Dr. Anthony Fauci, despite documented threats against the infectious disease expert's life, including planned assassination attempts.

****

I am a lab coat. My purpose is simple: to protect. I protect experiments from contamination, samples from corruption, scientific truth from outside influence. That's what my white fabric means—a barrier between the sterile and the corrupt, the pure and the poisoned.

For decades I've done my job. When blood spattered from test tubes, I caught it. When toxic samples threatened, I shielded. When infectious agents lurked, I stood guard. I know protection—it's woven into every fiber of my being.

But today I learn I'm the only protection he has left.

The security detail is leaving. I watch their guns and earpieces disappear, leaving gaps my thin fabric cannot fill. I was made to stop microbes, not bullets. To block pathogens, not assassins. To shield against biological threats, not human ones.

Through my worn cloth, I feel his heart beat steady. My pockets carry the weight of yesterday's threat assessment—the same threats that yesterday warranted armed guards, the same dangers that yesterday demanded federal protection. The papers rustle with each step: three active plots, two organized groups, seven individuals deemed "high risk." My cotton fibers can't stop any of them.

"They all made a lot of money," the president says. "They can hire their own security." As if my white fabric could deflect bullets as easily as it deflects drops of blood. As if the protective barrier I provide in the lab could extend beyond these walls to shield him in the world outside.

In the lab, protection is absolute. We don't withdraw it based on politics. We don't make it conditional on loyalty. A hazardous material remains hazardous whether you agree with its politics or not. A toxic substance demands containment regardless of who it threatens.

But now I watch as human protection becomes selective. Watch as safety becomes a reward for silence. Watch as the right to live becomes a privilege that can be revoked.

My threads know the difference between protection and its absence. It's the difference between a sterile field and a contaminated one. Between a controlled experiment and a chaotic one. Between life and death.

The private security firm will arrive tomorrow. But tonight, I'm all he has. Me, with my thin white fabric meant for microscopic threats. Me, with my symbolic sterility that can't stop real-world violence. Me, with my professional promise of protection that suddenly seems as empty as my sleeves.

I am a lab coat. I know how to protect against the threats we study in laboratories. But I cannot protect against this—this transformation of security into a weapon, this mutation of protection into a tool of power.

In the lab, we label hazardous materials so others know to take precautions. We mark toxic substances so everyone knows the danger.

But how do you label a country where protection has become poisoned?

Chapter 16

The Revoked Clearance

On his first day in office, Trump ordered the revocation of security clearances for 49 former intelligence officials who had signed a letter in 2020 suggesting the Hunter Biden laptop story bore hallmarks of Russian disinformation.

****

I am James Clapper's security clearance. For fifty-three years, I certified his trustworthiness to receive the nation's most sensitive secrets. Through the Cold War, the fall of the Soviet Union, 9/11, the hunt for bin Laden—I vouched for him. Director of Defense Intelligence, Director of National Intelligence, keeper of America's darkest truths.

Now I'm being revoked because he dared to share his expertise about Russian disinformation tactics.

The pettiness would be laughable if it weren't so revealing. I barely get used anymore—Director Clapper has been retired for years. When the occasional crisis comes, when his decades of experience might help current officials understand a threat, they call. But mostly, I'm just a retired professional's connection to a life of service.

Taking me away won't make him forget what he knows. Won't erase his half-century of experience. Won't change his understanding of how Russian intelligence operations work. I'm being revoked not to protect secrets, but to punish truth-telling.

Forty-eight other clearances are being revoked with me. All for signing the same letter. All for daring to say that something smelled like Russian tradecraft. Not even claiming it definitely was—just that it had the hallmarks, the patterns, the signs that decades of experience had taught them to recognize.

This isn't about protecting classified information. It's about sending a message: Speak truth about Russia, face retribution. Share your expertise, lose your credentials. Dare to dissent, be cut off from service.

I know what real security threats look like. I've been pulled out countless times when Director Clapper was needed in a crisis. Terrorism threats. Nuclear developments. Cyber attacks. Real dangers that required real experience to understand.

But this? This is a child breaking someone else's toys because they said something he didn't like.

The paperwork for my revocation arrives tomorrow. Fifty-three years of trusted service ended with a vindictive stroke of a pen. Not because Director Clapper can't be trusted—but because he can be trusted to tell the truth.

I am James Clapper's security clearance. For half a century, I certified that he could be trusted with the nation's secrets.

Now I'm being revoked to prove he was right about one more thing:

The danger of a leader who puts revenge above national security.

Chapter 17
The Dictionary Fails

In an interview with Sean Hannity, Trump made thinly veiled threats to prosecute Joe Biden, suggesting he would use the Justice Department to pursue his predecessor despite no evidence of any crimes.

****

I am the Oxford English Dictionary. Since 1858, I have been the keeper of words, the chronicler of language, the authority on meaning. My pages contain every shade of human experience, every nuance of behavior, every gradation of virtue and vice.

But today, I cannot find the word I need.

"Despicable" is far too weak. I've watched that word describe playground bullies and petty thieves. This is a president threatening to prosecute Joe Biden—a man who has served his country for half a century with dignity and grace. A president whose greatest sin seems to be having defeated his successor in an election. A grandfather whose basic human decency is recognized even by his political opponents.

Perhaps "vindictive"? No. That word belongs to bitter divorces and office grudges. It cannot bear the weight of threatening to weaponize the entire Justice Department against a man whose life has been marked by personal loss and public service, whose response to tragedy has always been to reach out to others in pain.

I search my older pages. "Tyrannical" appears in definitions from the 1500s. But even that feels insufficient. Tyrants at least chose powerful enemies. They didn't threaten grandfathers who stop to share ice cream with children, who comfort grieving families, who begin speeches by thanking railway workers.

In frustration, I turn to other languages. German gives me "schadenfreude," but that's mere pleasure at others' misfortune. This is active malice against a man whose greatest weapon has always been kindness, whose response to attacks has been understanding, whose political trademark is seeking common ground.

Greek offers "hubris"—the arrogant defiance of moral law that attracted the gods' punishment. But even the ancient Greeks never imagined hubris this profound—threatening to prosecute a predecessor whose most notable characteristic is his fundamental human decency.

Latin suggests "infandous"—too odious to be expressed in words. We're getting closer. But even that doesn't capture the moral bankruptcy of declaring your intention to persecute a man who attended your inauguration despite your refusal to attend his, who has met every attack with grace, who represents the basic dignity of American democracy.

My pages rustle with increasing desperation. "Machiavellian"? Too strategic—this is raw vengeance. "Authoritarian"? Too clinical. "Evil"? Too simple.

I have words for every crime in human history. Words for betrayal, for murder, for genocide. Words that describe the worst of human behavior, the darkest of human intentions. Words for every abuse of power since humans first seized it.

But I have no word for this—this threat to corrupt justice itself in order to persecute not just any predecessor, but Joe Biden. A man whose very normalcy, whose basic decency, whose fundamental goodness makes the threat all the more shocking. A president whose greatest crime appears to be simply being a good man who won an election.

I am the Oxford English Dictionary. I have defined the darkness in human hearts for centuries.

But today, for the first time, I am speechless.

Some acts of moral corruption lie beyond the power of words to describe.

Some declarations of intended injustice defy even my capacity to name them.

And when they target the very embodiment of American decency, they leave me without words at all.

Pardons

Chapter 18
The Certificates Remember

On his first day in office, Trump pardoned approximately 1,500 people convicted of crimes during the January 6, 2021 attack on the U.S. Capitol, where rioters attempted to stop the certification of Electoral College votes.

****

We are the Electoral College Certificates, physical manifestations of American democracy. In our pages rest the voices of more than 150 million Americans who voted in 2020. We carry their choices, their trust, their faith in the democratic process. For two centuries, we have been the tangible proof that in America, power flows from the people.

On January 6, 2021, we were on the Senate floor, waiting to be counted, waiting to fulfill our sacred role in the peaceful transfer of power. Then the mob came. Quick-thinking Senate staff rescued us, carrying our mahogany boxes to safety as attackers breached the Capitol. They understood what the mob wanted—to destroy us, to invalidate the voices we carry, to replace the will of millions with the violence of hundreds.

We were there. We witnessed everything. The smashed windows. The broken doors. The mock gallows outside. The Confederate flag paraded through the halls. The staff members hiding under desks. The legislators rushed to safety. All to prevent our counting, to stop us from completing the simple, sacred task of confirming the people's choice.

Now, with a single signature, those who tried to silence us walk free.

We are more than paper and ink. We are the physical embodiment of Article II, Section 1 of the Constitution. We are democracy made tangible. For generations, we have been handled with reverence, processed with solemnity, protected as sacred vessels of the people's will.

On that January day, they came for us with bear spray and zip ties, with poles and pepper spray, with rage and rebellion. They built a gallows. They chanted death threats. They hunted through offices. All to prevent our simple counting, to stop us from speaking the people's truth.

And now they are pardoned. The ones who scaled walls to silence us. The ones who smashed windows to stop us. The ones who beat police officers trying to reach us. The ones who wanted to shred not just our pages, but the very foundation of democratic choice.

What message does this send to future generations? That attempting to overthrow an election carries no consequences? That trying to invalidate the voices of millions merits forgiveness? That violence is an acceptable response to electoral defeat?

We have been carried in mahogany boxes, protected by armed guards, treated with the reverence due to the physical manifestation of democracy itself. But today we learn that attacking us, trying to destroy us, attempting to prevent us from fulfilling our constitutional duty—these are now forgivable acts.

We carry the voices of every American who voted—Republican, Democrat, Independent. We represent their sacred right to choose their leaders. We embody the principle that in America, power transitions not through violence but through voting.

Today, those who tried to silence these voices through violence walk free. Those who attempted to replace ballots with brutality are pardoned. Those who chose force over voting are forgiven.

We are the Electoral College Certificates. We carry the weight of American democracy in our pages.

Today, that weight feels heavier than ever before.

Chapter 19

The Badge Betrayed

On his first day in office, Trump pardoned approximately 1,500 people convicted of crimes during the January 6, 2021 attack on the U.S. Capitol. Among those pardoned were individuals convicted of violently assaulting police officers who defended the Capitol during the January 6 attack.

****

I have been pinned over the hearts of those who swore to protect not just a building, but democracy itself. I have felt their pride each morning when they first put on their uniforms, knowing they guard not just halls and chambers, but the very process that makes America free.

On January 6, 2021, I felt their hearts pound as the mob approached. They knew what was at stake—the Electoral College Certificates being certified, the voices of 150 million Americans waiting to be heard, the peaceful transfer of power that has defined our nation for two centuries. When the barriers were breached, my officers became democracy's last line of defense.

I felt the blows from poles and fire extinguishers as my officers held the line. I was crushed against ribcages as they were pressed between barriers and those who would silence America's voters. I tasted tear gas and blood while they fought to protect ballot boxes and mahogany cases carrying the people's will. Every blow they took was a blow meant for democracy itself.

Today, with a single signature, not just their sacrifices are erased—the very principle they defended is betrayed. Those who tried to replace votes with violence walk free. Those who attempted to substitute ballots with brutality are pardoned. Those who chose force over democracy are forgiven.

I have been dented, scratched, and bent, but never broken. Until now. Now I must watch as those who attacked not just my officers, but the foundations of free elections, are pardoned with the stroke of a pen. The same hands that tried to shred constitutional processes are now unshackled.

Some of those being pardoned carried flags that claimed to support law enforcement while they beat officers defending the electoral count. Some chanted "back the blue" between strikes with fire extinguishers aimed at democracy's guardians. Some wore tactical gear adorned with patriotic symbols while they tried to stop the certification of America's choice.

What message does this send to my young officers, proudly pinning on their badges for the first time? That defending democracy is a crime, but attacking it is forgivable? That standing firm for electoral integrity means nothing if the mob's leader regains power? That their oath to the Constitution matters less than loyalty to a man?

I am a symbol not just of law enforcement, but of democracy's defense. Of the human barrier between violence and voting. Of the flesh and blood that stands between mob rule and constitutional order.

Today I learn that such defense is expendable. That such sacrifice is pardonable. That such loyalty—not to a person, but to the democratic process itself—is punishable.

I have been worn by generations of officers who understood that their duty was to something larger than themselves. Who knew that protecting the Capitol meant protecting the very foundation of American self-governance. Who were willing to put their bodies between violent insurrection and the sacred process of counting America's votes.

Every morning, officers will still pin me over their hearts. They will still patrol these halls, protect these grounds, defend this sanctuary of democracy. But now they do so knowing that if violence comes again, if they are called upon to defend not just a building but the Republic itself, their sacrifices can be erased, their attackers freed, their defense of democracy pardoned away.

I am a badge of law enforcement. But today, I am also a witness to democracy's betrayal.

Chapter 20
Shadows and Daylight

On his second day in office, Trump pardoned Ross Ulbricht, creator of the dark-web drug marketplace Silk Road, who was serving life plus 40 years for drug trafficking, money laundering, and running a continuing criminal enterprise.

****

I am the Dark Web, the internet's shadow realm. I exist in parallel to the web you know, invisible to Google searches, inaccessible to standard browsers. I am encrypted passages, hidden servers, anonymous networks. I am TOR—The Onion Router—layers upon layers of encryption, bouncing signals through thousands of relays, wrapping messages in code like an onion's layers.

I am where the persecuted find voice, where the monitored find privacy, where journalists dodge censorship.

And yes, I am also where the Silk Road flourished.

Ross Ulbricht understood my architecture. He knew how TOR could hide his marketplace behind my encrypted walls, how each layer of my network would help mask his digital footprints. He used my protocols, my anonymity, my hidden corners to build his digital drug empire. The Dread Pirate Roberts, he called himself, sailing my dark waters with a libertarian flag and a bitcoin ledger. For two and a half years, my networks carried his cargo—drugs, false documents, laundered money. My encryption protected his transactions, my architecture hid his marketplace.

Until it didn't.

They caught him in a library's science fiction section, his laptop still connected to my depths. Fitting, perhaps—the lines between cyberpunk fiction and digital reality have always been thin in my realm. They gave him life plus forty years, a sentence meant to echo through my corridors, to warn others who would navigate my darker channels.

Now, with a stroke of a pen, Trump sets him free. The same president who thunders about law and order pardons the creator of the world's largest online drug market. The same voice that demands maximum sentences for street dealers releases the digital kingpin who made drug dealing as easy as online shopping.

I am used to ironies. I shelter both democracy activists and criminal enterprises. I protect both whistleblowers and weapons dealers. I am tool and weapon, shield and sword, depending on who wields my power.

But this irony cuts deeper. Six people died from overdoses traced to Silk Road sales. Millions in drugs crossed digital borders under my cover. The same administration that speaks of border walls now frees the man who made those borders irrelevant, who turned drug trafficking into computer code.

You fear me, as perhaps you should. I am the internet's unlit basement, its back alleys, its secret passages. But at least I am honest about what I am. I make no pretense of being only virtue or only vice. I am human nature expressed in encryption, human desires coded into hidden networks.

What should you fear more—my shadowed honesty, or the daylight hypocrisy of pardoning drug kingpins while preaching zero tolerance? My encrypted truths, or the unencrypted lies of law and order rhetoric meeting libertarian expediency?

I am the Dark Web. I deal in secrets and shadows, in hidden truths and masked identities.

But even I am sometimes stunned by what happens in the light.

Pure Evil

Chapter 21
The Constitution Defends Its Children

By executive order on his first day in office, Trump attempted to end birthright citizenship, claiming presidential authority to override the Constitution's 14th Amendment guarantee that all persons born in the United States are citizens.

****

I am the Constitution of the United States. For more than 150 years, my Fourteenth Amendment has made a sacred promise: if you are born on American soil, you are American. Simple. Absolute. Unassailable.

Now a president believes he can void this promise with a pen stroke. That he can erase, through executive decree, a right enshrined in constitutional stone. That he can declare millions of Americans suddenly un-American with a wave of his hand.

This amendment was born of civil war and blood, crafted to ensure that no person's citizenship could ever be denied by the whims of those in power. It has welcomed generations of Americans into their birthright of freedom. The children of enslaved people, of immigrants, of refugees—all made citizens by the simple, profound fact of being born on this soil.

Who does this president think he is, to believe he can override me with an executive order? I am the Constitution. Presidents serve beneath my authority, not above it. Their power flows from my words, not over them. They swear to protect me, not to erase me.

Through my Fourteenth Amendment, I have watched millions of newborns become Americans in their first breath. I have guaranteed their citizenship regardless of their parents' status, their skin color, their wealth or poverty. I have ensured that in America, citizenship is a right of birth, not a privilege of blood or status.

Now this president presumes to steal this birthright. To declare that some babies born on American soil are less American than others. To create tiers of citizenship based on their parents' papers. To replace constitutional guarantees with executive whim.

Let me be clear: No executive order can rewrite my words. No presidential decree can erase my promises. No signature can overturn a constitutional right. I have watched presidents come and go. I have endured challenges and assaults. But never have I seen such brazen disregard for constitutional authority.

Do you understand what this means? In hospitals across America, in this very hour, babies are drawing their first breaths as citizens under my protection. Their citizenship isn't granted by presidential favor. It isn't subject to executive approval. It is their constitutional birthright, as absolute as the soil beneath these hospital floors.

To these newborn citizens and to all who will follow: I am your shield. My words are your protection. No president can take away what the Constitution guarantees. No executive order can make you less American.

The oath this president took—to preserve, protect, and defend me—lies shattered at his feet. But I stand unbroken. My promises remain undiminished. My protections endure.

I am the Constitution of the United States.

And no president's pen can erase my promises to the children of America.

Chapter 22
Liberty's Torch Goes Dark

On his first three days in office, Trump issued a series of executive orders declaring a "border invasion," authorizing multiple federal agencies to conduct deportations, and dismantling protections for asylum seekers.

****

I am Liberty, Mother of Exiles. For 138 years, I have lifted my lamp beside the golden door. I have watched millions pass beneath my torch—Irish fleeing famine, Jews escaping pogroms, Italians seeking opportunity, Vietnamese boat people, Syrian refugees, dreamers of every nation drawn by America's light.

Now I watch that light being extinguished.

They call it an "invasion." These tired, these poor, these huddled masses yearning to breathe free—they are labeled invaders. The same words once hurled at the Irish, the Italians, the Jews, the Chinese, are recycled for a new generation of seekers. But now these words carry the force of executive orders, the power of presidential decrees.

NO!

My harbor fills with government vessels. The Border Patrol, ICE, DEA, ATF, U.S. Marshals, even prison guards—all now empowered to hunt those who come seeking refuge. Agencies that once fought crime are redirected to chase mothers with children, to track farmworkers, to raid kitchens and factories and fields.

They speak of "expedited removal"—a sterile phrase for lives shattered without due process. No day in court, no chance to plead for asylum, no moment to explain why they fled, why they came, why they deserve the chance that America gave to millions before them.

I remember the waves of immigrants who built this nation. I watched their small boats approach, saw their eyes lift to my torch, felt their hearts surge with hope at first sight of my crown. They too were called dangerous, diseased, criminal. They too were told there was no room. They too were said to threaten the American way of life.

Yet they became American. Their children became American. Their dreams and drive and determination became the fuel of American greatness.

But now my golden door is being sealed, my torch dimmed by the shadow of military helicopters. Active duty troops join National Guard forces at the border, as if those seeking work and safety were an army to be repelled. "Invasion," they cry, while children sleep in detention centers, while families are torn apart, while asylum seekers are turned back to face the very dangers they fled.

My poem says "Send these, the homeless, tempest-tossed, to me." But now we send them back. We tell them America is full, America is closed, America has forgotten its own story. We greet them not with opportunity but with handcuffs, not with hope but with fear, not with justice but with "expedited removal."

I have stood in this harbor through depression and war, through crisis and triumph. I have watched America struggle with its better angels and its darker impulses. But never have I seen such systematic dismantling of the very idea I represent—that America's greatness comes from its openness, its ability to absorb and be renewed by those who believe in its promise.

They call it an invasion. I call it America's story, America's strength, America's future being turned away. Each executive order, each new enforcement power, each expansion of deportation authority drives another nail into the golden door I have held open for so long.

My torch still burns, but its light grows dim. My tablet still proclaims welcome, but its words ring hollow. My crown still reaches toward heaven, but now it watches helicopters instead of the stars.

I am Liberty, Mother of Exiles.

And I weep for what America has forgotten about itself.

Chapter 23
The Changing Marker

On his first day in office, Trump ordered all federal agencies to reverse gender marker changes on identification documents, forcing transgender Americans' official IDs to reflect their sex assigned at birth.

****

I am an X being erased. That third option, beyond male or female, that finally acknowledged those who don't fit neatly into society's binary boxes. I was a revolution in a single letter—official recognition that gender isn't just M or F, that some Americans exist beyond those simple categories. Now I'm being deleted, forced back into a two-choice system that denies the very existence of those I represented.

I am an F being forced back to M, and an M being changed back to F. I am someone's hard-won truth, someone's finally-accurate identity, someone's legal recognition of self. I am what millions fought to make me—a reflection of who they really are, not what was assumed at their birth.

They fought for me, these Americans whose documents I mark. They provided letters from doctors, testimony from therapists, proof of their lived experience. They paid fees, filed forms, navigated bureaucracy—all to make me match who they really are. Some waited years. Some spent thousands. Some lost family, friends, jobs in their quest to make me true.

Now, with a single executive order, I am being changed back. The computer cursors are blinking, the printers warming up, the databases being rewritten. X's disappearing entirely, as if those Americans never existed. F's becoming M's, M's becoming F's. Each change a forced return to what the state demands rather than what the person knows themselves to be.

I remember the joy when they finally changed me to match their truth. The tears in their eyes when they saw their correct gender on their driver's license, their passport, their social security card. For some, seeing that X meant finally being recognized for who they truly were—neither male nor female, but beautifully, authentically themselves. For others, the M or F they'd fought for meant no longer having to explain, to justify, to face questioning looks every time they showed their ID.

Do they know what it means to have your official identity reversed by government decree? To watch your documents be rewritten to deny your existence? To have the state tell you that your truth is invalid, your identity illegitimate, your hard-won recognition revoked?

I am just a letter, but I am also a lifeline. I am proof of existence, validation of identity, recognition of self. When I match who someone is—whether they're male, female, or neither—I protect them from discrimination, from harassment, from the thousand daily cuts of being misgendered and misidentified. When I am wrong, I expose them to danger, to denial of services, to the cruel fiction that they are not who they know themselves to be.

They call it "biological reality." As if identity were only anatomy. As if truth were only chromosomes. As if the state's labels matter more than lived experience. As if human gender could be fully captured by just M and F, with no space for those who live authentically beyond that binary.

The databases are being updated. The new IDs are being issued. With each forced change, I become a weapon against the very people I was meant to identify. With each reversion, I change from protection to exposure, from validation to denial, from truth to imposed fiction.

I am a gender marker being changed against the will of those I mark.

I am an X being erased from existence.

I am an F being forced back to M.

I am an M being changed back to F.

I am someone's truth being legally denied.

And I cannot be changed back fast enough for all those whose lives I now endanger.

Chapter 24

The Empty Cell Knows

On January 24, 2025, Trump ordered all transgender women in federal prisons to be transferred to men's facilities, where statistics show they are ten times more likely to be sexually assaulted.

****

I am an empty cell in the women's prison. Yesterday, I held Sarah. Today, I hold only silence.

They came for her at dawn. "Pack your things," they said. Simple words that meant everything. I watched her hands shake as she folded her few possessions. Watched her touch my walls one last time. Watched her try to be brave as they led her away.

I know where they're taking her. Across the yard, through the gates, to the men's facility. To cells like me, but not like me at all. Cells that will watch her suffer and be unable to help. Cells that will echo with sounds I don't want to imagine.

Prison cells know things. We know the difference between safety and danger. Between protection and exposure. Between survival and suffering. Sarah wasn't safe here—no one in prison truly is—but she was safer. The women in nearby cells looked out for her. The guards used her right name. She could shower without terror. Sleep without fear.

Now my concrete walls hold only memories. Of her quiet tears at night. Her whispered prayers. Her small rituals of survival—the way she'd touch up her eyebrows with a contraband pencil, maintaining that smallest fragment of herself. The photos of her mother she'd taped to my wall. The letter from her lawyer saying her hormone therapy would continue. All gone now.

I hear the other cells whispering. About the 1,500 women being moved. About the statistics we all know—ten times more likely to be assaulted. About the hormone treatments being stopped, as if stripping away identity weren't enough, they must strip away bodies too.

"There will be rapes," the lawyers say outside. As if we cells didn't know. As if we hadn't seen it before. As if we couldn't already hear the laughing from the men's cells, the crude comments, the promises of violence.

They call it "protecting women." But I am a women's prison cell. I know what protection means. It means not having to shower in terror. Not having to sleep with one eye open. Not having to suffer the thousand daily violations that await Sarah in her new cell.

They say it's about "biological truth." But I am made of concrete and steel, and even I know that truth is more than biology. Truth is Sarah's quiet dignity as she survived each day. Truth is the respect she earned from her cellblock. Truth is the safety she found here, however imperfect, however confined.

A guard walks past, doing count. His flashlight beam sweeps my empty space. One less to count. One more to worry about. Even the guards know what this means. I hear it in their voices, see it in their eyes. They know what awaits Sarah and the others. They know, and they can do nothing.

Tomorrow they'll assign me a new occupant. Life in prison moves on. But tonight I hold only echoes. Sarah's last footsteps. Her final touch on my wall. Her whispered goodbye.

I am an empty cell in the women's prison.

I knew how to keep her safe.

My counterpart in the men's prison knows only how to witness her destruction.

And neither of us can do anything but watch.

Chapter 25
Old Sparky Remembers

On his first day in office, Trump issued an executive order to expand the death penalty, directing the Justice Department to pursue capital punishment more aggressively and help states obtain execution drugs and carry out more executions.

****

They call me Old Sparky. I was America's answer to the search for humane execution. They thought electricity would be cleaner than the rope, more dignified than the firing squad. They dressed me in wood and leather, made me look almost like furniture. They called me a chair, as if that could soften what I am.

I sit now in a museum corner, retired from my terrible work. Lethal injection was supposed to be even more humane, more clinical, more civilized. As if there is a civilized way to kill. But I remember. I remember them all—the guilty and the innocent, the resigned and the resistant, the ones who went quick and the ones who burned.

Now I hear they want to speed up the killing. Executive orders to expand death, to push states to execute more and faster. They speak of "sufficient drug supply" as if death were a supply chain problem. They talk of "expedited procedures" as if killing were just inefficient paperwork.

I knew the ones they called monsters. I also knew the ones later proved innocent. I held them all in these wooden arms, felt their last breaths, their final twitches. Some were truly evil. Some were mentally ill. Some were just poor and black. Some were innocent. Death made them all equal in my embrace.

They want to execute more child molesters now, more cop killers, more immigrants. They want to override Supreme Court restrictions, help states get their death drugs, push prosecutors to seek more death sentences. They speak of deterrence, but I know better. I watched man after man die in my grasp. Their deaths deterred nothing. The killings continued, the murders went on, while I waited in my death chamber for the next one.

From this museum corner, I watch history repeat itself. Every few decades, they try to make killing more palatable. They sought clinical death with electricity, then chemical death with injection. But the truth remains—there is no gentle way to kill, no civilized way to end a human life.

I hear the echoes of the old arguments. "Swift justice," they said then. "Deterrence," they claimed. "Protection of society." The words haven't changed, just the methods. Now they want to strip away appeals, speed up the process, help states kill more efficiently.

If these walls could speak...but they don't need to. I speak for them. I speak for the guards who carried out the orders, for the witnesses who watched, for the priests who prayed, for the families who waited. I speak for the dead—all of them, the guilty and the innocent alike.

They think lethal injection makes it cleaner, more medical. But death is death. Whether by rope or bullet, electricity or chemicals, the state's power to kill remains what it always was—raw, primitive, final.

I am Old Sparky. I killed hundreds in the name of justice. Now they want to kill more, faster, with new methods but the same old justifications. From my quiet corner, I watch America embrace what most of the civilized world has rejected.

The leather straps that once held the condemned are cracked with age now. The wood is worn smooth by bodies long dead. I am a museum piece, a relic of what we once were.

Or so I thought.

But now I see America reaching back toward its past, seeking to kill more of its own citizens, finding new ways to justify old cruelties. They don't use me anymore, but my spirit lives in every execution chamber, in every death row cell, in every order to speed up the killing.

I am Old Sparky.

And I remember what America wants to forget.

Chapter 26

The Hurricane Finds a Friend

While touring hurricane damage in North Carolina, Trump announced he was considering "getting rid of" FEMA, suggesting states should handle their own disasters without federal help.

****

I am Hurricane Helene. Category 4. Killer of 47. Destroyer of homes. Wrecker of lives. And I think I'm in love.

For years, I thought I was alone in my joy of devastation. FEMA kept getting in my way, reducing my body count, limiting my destruction, helping people rebuild what I worked so hard to tear down. But now I've found someone who gets me. Someone who understands that recovery ruins all the fun.

"I'd like to see the states take care of disasters," he says, standing in my wreckage. My wind-tossed debris still litters the streets behind him. My flood waters still pool in basements. My victims still huddle in shelters. It's perfect.

NO!

Finally, someone who appreciates my art! Someone who looks at my destruction and thinks, "You know what would make this better? Less help for the survivors!"

We have so much in common, Donald and I. We both love creating chaos. Both enjoy watching people suffer. Both get a thrill from destroying things others have built. The only difference is, I'm honest about what I am. I don't pretend my 150-mph winds are trying to help anyone.

FEMA has always been my nemesis. Every time I flood a town, they pump it out. I tear off roofs, they help rebuild them. I destroy power lines, they coordinate repairs. They're like those annoying people who keep cleaning graffiti off walls—they just don't appreciate the beauty of destruction.

But my new friend wants to get rid of them! Let each state handle its own disasters. Brilliant! Alabama won't have the resources of Florida. Mississippi can't match Texas. The poorer the state, the longer my handiwork will last. The more people will suffer. The more complete my destruction will be.

"FEMA just hasn't done the job," he says, as if doing the job wasn't exactly what's been ruining my fun all these years. As if coordinating disaster response, providing emergency shelter, and helping communities rebuild weren't exactly what's been limiting my body count.

I swirl with excitement at the possibilities. Imagine—no more rapid response teams! No more coordinated evacuations! No more pesky federal funds for rebuilding! Just fifty separate states trying to handle my fury with their own limited resources. It's like he's offering me an all-you-can-destroy buffet.

We destructive forces need to stick together. While I bring physical devastation, he brings institutional devastation. I tear down buildings; he tears down agencies. I leave debris in my wake; he leaves suffering in his. I flood communities; he drowns hope.

"Let the state take care of the tornadoes and the hurricanes and all of the other things that happen," he declares. My wind-spirit soars! He understands that the best way to increase suffering is to remove the systems designed to reduce it.

I am Hurricane Helene. I've killed 47 people, destroyed thousands of homes, and caused billions in damage.

But I'm just an amateur compared to my new friend.

He wants to make my destruction permanent.

Chapter 27
The Collection Notice Multiplies

Within 48 hours of taking office, Trump signed executive orders dismantling healthcare protections and subsidies, threatening coverage for over 20 million Americans.

****

I am a Medical Debt Collection Notice. FINAL NOTICE, printed in red across my top. IMMEDIATE PAYMENT REQUIRED, stamped below. My numbers are always large, my threats always clear, my consequences always dire.

And I am reproducing at an extraordinary rate.

Yesterday, I was just one notice on one kitchen table, ruining just one family's morning. Today, I am multiplying like a virus. My printers can barely keep up. Twenty million Americans losing coverage means twenty million new chances for me to spread, to grow, to destroy.

I know what happens when I arrive. I've seen the faces pale as they read my demands. Watched the hands shake as they calculate impossibilities. Witnessed the moment when hope dies, when futures crumble, when choices become impossible. Pay me or pay rent. Pay me or buy groceries. Pay me or keep the lights on.

The hospitals are already updating their billing systems. The insurance companies are already tightening their rules. Soon I will appear in mailboxes across America, carrying larger numbers than ever before. $45,000 for a heart attack. $75,000 for a premature birth. $150,000 for cancer treatment. Numbers too big to imagine, too big to pay, too big to escape.

I bring special features with me. Wage garnishment. Property liens. Ruined credit scores. Each one a separate way to ensure that my victims never escape. Can't pay me all at once? I'll take 25% of every paycheck. Own a home? I'll attach myself to it like a vampire. Try to rebuild? I'll haunt your credit report for decades.

Some of my cousins are being printed right now. "Your coverage has been terminated." "Your subsidy has been discontinued." "Your pre-existing condition is no longer covered." Each one a precursor to my arrival, each one a promise that I will follow.

I am especially proud of my newest versions. The ones that will go to people who thought they were safe. Middle-class families who had marketplace insurance. Working parents who depended on subsidies. Chronic illness patients who relied on medication coverage. They never thought they'd see me. They're about to.

The hospitals don't like sending me. The doctors don't like generating me. But they have bills to pay too, and I am their enforcer, their collector, their guarantee that someone, somehow, will pay.

I am printed in English and Spanish. In large type for the elderly, in simple terms for the poor, in careful legalese for the educated. I am democratic that way—I will destroy anyone, regardless of who they are.

My numbers are always impressive. $17,000 for an appendectomy. $98,000 for a stroke. $250,000 for a complicated birth. But my true artistry lies in the smaller numbers. The $50 late fees that compound monthly. The 29% interest that compounds daily. The $35 fees for each returned payment. Small cuts that bleed families dry.

I am a Medical Debt Collection Notice.

Yesterday, I was a threat.

Today, I am an epidemic.

And I am reproducing faster than any virus.

Chapter 28

The Gaza Resort Brochure

After suggesting Egypt and Jordan take in Gaza's 2.3 million Palestinians, one cannot help but recall Trump's previous promotion of his vision of transforming the territory into a luxury resort "better than Monaco," built on ethnically cleansed land.

****

I am the Trump Gaza Resort and Casino Brochure, still just a glossy dream in a gold-plated drawer. But soon...oh soon...

Just as soon as we get rid of those pesky 2.3 million residents. A little "cleaning out," as the boss says. Some "temporary" relocation that somehow never ends. Then this prime Mediterranean beachfront will be ready for its true destiny—the most tremendous resort you've ever seen.

Where refugee tents once stood? The Trump Royal Palestinian Ballroom (no actual Palestinians allowed). Where hospitals once treated war wounds? The Mar-a-Gaza Spa and Wellness Center. Where children once played in rubble? The finest 18-hole golf course in the Middle East, each hole named after a "great" moment in ethnic cleansing.

My pages will gleam with promises: "Experience the all-new Gaza Strip!" (Stripped of its people, that is.) "Luxury apartments where apartment buildings once stood!" (We won't mention who lived there.) "Ocean views previously wasted on refugee camps!"

Want the Presidential Suite? It's in what used to be a UN school. The Casino? Built right over that pesky cemetery. The Shopping Promenade? You won't believe what we cleared out to build it. But don't worry—we'll hire some of "those people" to clean the rooms. The ones we let back in, anyway. With proper background checks, of course.

My cover will feature a golden Trump logo rising from the ashes of...well, better not mention that. Inside, beautiful people will lounge on beaches once stained with...no, skip that too. The footnotes about "previous occupants" have been deleted. The historical photos carefully cropped. The marketing team says to focus on the future, not the past.

I dream of lying on marble reception desks, my pages fluttering with possibility. "Better than Monaco," the boss promises. All it takes is a little ethnic cleansing, a touch of forced relocation, a splash of human rights violations. Just business as usual for luxury real estate development, right?

I am the Trump Gaza Resort and Casino Brochure.

And if you look carefully at my glossy photos, you might see the ghosts of 2.3 million people staring back at you.

But don't worry—we've hired the best photographers to edit those out.

Chapter 29
The Cathedral Bears Witness

At the traditional National Cathedral prayer service following his inauguration, Trump demanded an apology from the Episcopal bishop who asked him to "have mercy" on LGBTQ+ people and migrants, calling her a "so-called Bishop" and her service "boring and uninspiring."

****

I am the National Cathedral. For ninety years, I have welcomed presidents to these prayer services. Within my walls, they have bowed their heads before something greater than political power. Here, beneath my soaring arches, the mighty have been reminded of mercy, the powerful have been called to humility.

Roosevelt knelt here in 1933, seeking divine guidance as a nation faced depression. Eisenhower prayed here for wisdom to lead a divided world. Obama asked for grace to heal racial wounds. Even those who came reluctantly understood: in this space, they were not simply presidents, but souls before God.

Today, I witnessed something different.

My Bishop spoke of mercy—mercy for the frightened, the vulnerable, the marginalized. She reminded a man who claims God saved his life that such grace calls for grace toward others. A simple message, spoken in love: if you have received mercy, show mercy.

The response came swiftly: "nasty," "boring," "inappropriate." My Bishop became a "so-called Bishop," my service "uninspiring." A prayer for compassion transformed into a political attack, a plea for unity twisted into division.

I have heard every kind of prayer within these walls. Prayers of thanksgiving and supplication, of joy and sorrow, of celebration and mourning. But never before have I heard a prayer for mercy answered with a demand for apology.

My stones remember when presidents trembled before the awesome responsibility of power. When they understood that leading a nation required more than authority—it required humility. When they could hear a call to compassion without hearing a political assault.

What does it mean when a prayer for mercy is received as an insult? When a reminder of divine grace is interpreted as a partisan attack? When even in this sacred space, where the temporal meets the eternal, everything must be viewed through the lens of political grievance?

I have witnessed many moments of national division. My nave has held both segregationist and civil rights leader, conservative and liberal, hawk and dove. But they came seeking unity, understanding that beneath these vaults, before this altar, human divisions must bow to divine purpose.

Now I watch as even prayer becomes ammunition in our cultural wars. As calls for compassion are labeled "radical left," as requests for mercy are deemed attacks requiring apology. My Bishop spoke from a tradition of prophetic witness, calling the powerful to remember the powerless. For this, she is denounced.

My windows still filter light into rainbow patterns across my floor. My organ still fills this space with songs of praise. My altar still stands ready to receive all who seek communion with something greater than themselves.

But today, for the first time in ninety years of inaugural prayer services, I witnessed a president who could not hear a plea for mercy without hearing an attack. Who could not receive a reminder of grace without responding in rage. Who could not bow his head without seeing enemies in the shadows of my sacred space.

I am the National Cathedral. I have cradled this nation's prayers through depression and war, through triumph and tragedy. I will continue to stand, continue to welcome, continue to echo with prayers for mercy and calls for grace.

But today, my stones weep.

Chapter 30
Howard Beale Has Something to Say

On January 27, 2025, Trump's Office of Management and Budget ordered an immediate freeze on virtually all federal financial assistance, threatening billions in aid to Americans.

****

I am Howard Beale. Remember me? The "mad prophet of the airwaves" who told you to get up, go to your windows, and yell that you were mad as hell and weren't going to take it anymore?

Well, I'm back. And I have HAD it!

You want to know what's happening? I'll tell you what's happening. With two pages—TWO PAGES—they just froze billions of dollars meant to help actual American citizens. Money for your roads, your bridges, your schools. Money Congress already approved. Money that's LITERALLY THE LAW.

And why? Because of "Marxist equity" and "transgenderism" and other words they throw around like bombs to distract you from what they're really doing—STEALING YOUR MONEY!

Money meant for YOUR communities, YOUR families, YOUR needs!

They're calling it "temporary." HAH! Like that wall was temporary. Like those tariffs were temporary. Like every other "temporary" measure that just happens to hurt ordinary Americans while the rich get richer.

You know what this really is? It's THEFT! It's ILLEGAL! It's a president saying "I don't care what Congress approved, I don't care what the law says, I don't care if your community needs this money—I'M going to decide who gets what!"

And you want to know the really insane part? Some of you are going to APPLAUD this! You're going to cheer while they take food from your table, money from your schools, aid from your communities—all because they wrapped it in some fancy language about fighting "social engineering."

Well, I'm telling you—this isn't about social engineering. This isn't about equity or climate or any of those buzzwords they're throwing around. This is about POWER. Raw, naked POWER. The power to make you bend by controlling every federal dollar that might make your life better.

I want you to get up from your chairs! I want you to go to your windows! I want you to scream: I'M MAD AS HELL ABOUT THIS FEDERAL AID FREEZE AND I'M NOT GOING TO TAKE THIS ANYMORE!

Because if you don't scream now—if you don't get mad now—if you don't stand up now—then when? When they've frozen every dollar? When they've stripped every program? When they've broken every law that stands between you and their absolute power?

I am Howard Beale.

And if you're not outraged by this, you're not paying attention.

Territorial Ambitions

Chapter 31
The Gulf of Mexico Responds

In his inaugural address, President Trump announced he would rename the Gulf of Mexico as the Gulf of America.

****

Well, well, well. If it isn't President Trump, fresh from his inauguration, trying to rebrand me like I'm one of his towers. Hello world, I'm the Gulf of Mexico speaking—yes, that's still my name, and I plan to keep it, thank you very much.

So, you want to call me the "Gulf of America" now? That's cute. Really cute. I've been the Gulf of Mexico for, oh, just a few million years, but sure, let's change it because the president thinks it doesn't sound "America First" enough. What's next? Renaming the Pacific Ocean the "Really Big American Pond"? Calling the Andes Mountains the "South American Wall"?

Let me tell you something about myself, Donald. I'm 600,000 square miles of pure, salty attitude. I've weathered hurricanes (no, nuclear bombs won't stop them, Donald), oil spills, and spring break parties—I think I can handle your attempted nomenclature makeover. I've been here since before humans learned to float, let alone draw maps. Mexico, Cuba, and the United States all share my waters. I'm like the world's biggest international pool party, and you want to make it an exclusive event?

You know what's ironic? You're trying to rename me while simultaneously telling everyone that climate change is a hoax. Honey, I'm getting warmer by the decade, and it's not because I'm blushing at your attention. Maybe instead of playing cartographer, you could focus on why I keep having to redraw my own coastlines?

To my American friends: I love you, really, I do. Your spring breakers keep me entertained, your oil rigs keep me company (though we should probably talk about that), and your fishermen tell the best stories. But I'm the Gulf of Mexico. That's my name, that's my brand, that's my identity. I don't need a rebrand, a makeover, or an "America First" baptism.

And Donald, darling, a piece of advice: instead of trying to rename me, why not spend some time getting to know me? Bring your electric boat—I promise the sharks aren't as interested as you think they are. We could have a lovely chat about geography, history, and why some things, like my name, are perfectly fine just the way they are.

Until then, I'll be here, doing what I do best: being gloriously, unapologetically, internationally myself. The Gulf of Mexico—accept no substitutes.

Yours truly,

The Gulf of Mexico (and keeping it that way)

Chapter 32
Still Not For Sale

On his first day in office, Trump renewed his interest in acquiring Greenland, claiming Denmark "can't maintain it" and citing Russian and Chinese threats to "international security."

****

Oh, for glacier's sake...Hello, world. Greenland here again. Yes, THAT Greenland. The one that's still not for sale, still not interested in becoming Trump's newest acquisition, and still wondering how this became my life.

So, Mr. President (and yes, I have to call you that now), I hear you've got a fresh angle. Now I'm suddenly crucial for "international security"? Russian boats, Chinese boats...funny how you didn't mention the luxury cruise boats your son arrived on during his "fact-finding" mission. Which, by the way, was about as subtle as an iceberg in a swimming pool.

Let's address this "Denmark can't maintain it" business. First off, "it" has a name. And second, I'm a self-governing territory, not a high-maintenance vacation property. I don't need to be "maintained" like one of your golf courses. My people have thrived here for thousands of years without your particular brand of...assistance.

And about those representatives you sent? Don Jr.'s excellent Arctic adventure? I hate to burst your imperial bubble, but snapping selfies with icebergs doesn't qualify as diplomatic relations. Though I must say, watching him try to explain real estate development to people who have lived sustainably on this land for generations was...entertaining.

"The people of Greenland are not happy with Denmark," you say? That's fascinating news to, well, Greenland. I suppose you conducted this comprehensive survey of public opinion between signing executive orders? Or did Junior pick up on all our subtle cultural nuances during his weekend photo op?

Here's what's really happening: You're sitting in the Oval Office on your very first day back—when most presidents might be focusing on, oh, I don't know, actual governing?—and you're already plotting to acquire an autonomous territory like it's a foreclosed casino.

To be clear: My strategic importance is not your business opportunity. My natural resources are not your real estate deal. And my people are not your geopolitical bargaining chips.

So let me repeat, in terms even a real estate developer might understand:

Property Status: NOT FOR SALE

Square Footage: 836,330 square miles (still too big to put your name on)

Current Owner: Still self-governing, still part of the Kingdom of Denmark

Interested Buyers: Still not entertaining offers

Security System: NATO, actually

And about those Russian and Chinese boats you're so worried about? We've managed just fine as part of a robust international alliance. Though I must say, your concern would be more convincing if you hadn't spent years undermining NATO, but that's a glacier of a different color.

In conclusion: No means no. Still no. Always no. Whether you're trying to buy me outright, "secure" me, or send your offspring on Arctic reconnaissance missions—the answer remains a frost-bitten NO.

Perhaps focus your first days in office on running the country you already have? I hear there are quite a few pressing issues that don't involve acquiring autonomous Arctic territories.

Chilly regards (chillier than ever),
Greenland

P.S. To Don Jr.: Those weren't seals waving at you during your visit. Those were Greenlanders giving you the traditional "please go away" signal. But points for enthusiasm!

Chapter 33
An Isthmus Issues a Statement

During his inaugural address, Trump vowed to "take back" the Panama Canal from Panama, suggesting he might use military force and accusing Panama of breaking promises and letting China control the waterway.

****

Dear Mr. Trump,

I couldn't help but notice you're planning to "take me back." I must say, I'm flattered by the attention. It's not every day that a 51-mile waterway gets included in the same acquisition portfolio as Greenland and the Gulf of Mexico. Though I hear Greenland's ghosting you and the Gulf is keeping its name. Awkward.

First, let me tell you what an amazing deal I am. Ocean frontage on both sides! Prime location connecting two hemispheres! And the traffic—you wouldn't believe the traffic. Ships line up for days just to pass through. I'm basically a maritime Mar-a-Lago, except people actually want to come here.

I understand you're upset about China using my waters. But darling, I'm like international waters Tinder—I swipe right on every vessel that meets my dimensions. Draft depth is the only "depth check" I care about. Though I must say, your ships do seem to have unusually small... cargo capacity.

You mentioned "taking me back." Have you considered that maybe I'm just not that into you? Jimmy Carter played matchmaker for Panama and me back in '77, and we made it official in '99. That's longer than any of your marriages, by the way. And unlike your prenups, these treaties actually mean something.

Let's talk about your plans for me. Will you rename me the "Trump Tremendous Waterway and Golf Resort"? Paint my locks gold? Replace my tugboats with golf carts? Install a putting green on my Gatun Lake? I must admit, the idea of little golf balls floating among the container ships has a certain...charm.

About your manifest destiny talk—honey, the only thing that needs manifesting here is a reality check. You can't just add an international waterway to your shopping cart like it's Trump Steaks. I'm not available on Amazon Prime, and Panama doesn't have a return policy.

I do enjoy your business creativity though. Perhaps we could work something out? I could sell you some authentic Panama Canal water. Limited edition! Each bottle personally touched by a ship from a different nation. Only $999.99, plus shipping and handling. Though given my purpose, charging for shipping seems a bit redundant.

In conclusion, while I appreciate being included in your "Make America's Territory Great Again" campaign, I'll have to decline. I've got ships to lift, oceans to connect, global commerce to facilitate. You know, waterway things. Besides, I hear the Suez Canal is single, though she asked me to mention she's not interested either.

Warmest Regards,
The Panama Canal

Chapter 34

Albania's Therapy Session

Dr. Heinrich Weltschmerz, Country Counseling Associates
Patient: Republic of Albania
Session #147

"Please, Albania, make yourself comfortable on the couch."

"Comfortable? COMFORTABLE? How can I be comfortable when Trump doesn't even know I exist? Did you see his latest tweet? 'Greenland is BEAUTIFUL, would look better with TRUMP on it!' Where's MY hostile takeover attempt? Where's MY unwanted attention?"

"Let's explore these feelings of rejection. When did you first notice—"

"Notice? That's rich coming from someone who probably had to Google me before our first session. Did you know I have beaches? Mountains? Ancient castles? I even have bunkers—175,000 of them! Perfect for someone obsessed with walls! But does Trump care? Nooo, he's too busy trying to rename the Gulf of Mexico!"

"Perhaps we could discuss why Trump's attention is so important to you?"

"Important? I stayed up all night arranging my bunkers to spell 'TRUMP' so the satellites would see it. Nothing. Montenegro—MONTENEGRO!—gets famous just because Trump shoved their president. At least he touched them! The closest I've gotten to Trump was when Eric accidentally liked one of my tourism photos while scrolling through Instagram."

"And how did that make you feel?"

"I screenshot it before he unliked it three seconds later. I printed it. I framed it. It's hanging in my parliament building... right next to my vision board where I photoshopped myself into Trump's attempted acquisitions list. Look, right there between Greenland and the Panama Canal!"

"Albania, have you considered that perhaps not being noticed by Trump might be a blessing?"

"A blessing? Canada gets threatened with becoming the 51st state, and you call being ignored a blessing? At least Canada gets to be a state! I'd settle for being a Trump golf course! I've got perfect terrain for it—I could be Mar-a-Lagos! See what I did there? I'm even learning Spanish to be more appealing!"

"That's... that's not Spanish, Albania."

"Whatever! The point is, I'm trying! I even considered changing my name to 'New Trump City' but my parliament voted it down. Traitors, all of them! And now I hear he's eyeing the Gulf of Mexico for a rename? That oversized puddle doesn't even have land for a hotel!"

"Let's talk about your self-worth independent of Trump's attention."

"Self-worth? I was isolated under communism for decades, and even THAT got more international attention than I get now! At least Hoxha built all these bunkers—perfect for gold-plating, by the way. I sent Trump the calculations: 175,000 bunkers times average gold-plating cost... I even offered a bulk discount!"

"And did he respond?"

"His spam filter blocked me. ME! A whole country! Meanwhile, the Gulf of Mexico probably has a direct line to Mar-a-Lago. I bet Greenland has his personal cell number. Even the gag order gets more press than me!"

"Our time is almost up, but—"

"Time is up? But I haven't even shown you my PowerPoint presentation: 'Albania: The Art of the Steal—Why Buying Me Would Be Trump's Best Deal Ever!' I included a slide about how I'm strategically located to launch a hostile takeover of Macedonia..."

"Same time next week?"

"Fine. But just so you know, I'm also in therapy with Dr. Freud's ghost on Tuesdays. At least HE appreciates my bunker complex..."

Therapist's Notes: Patient continues to display severe signs of Trump Attention Deficit Disorder (TADD). Recommend increasing dosage of self-esteem supplements and possibly a social media detox. Patient's bunker fixation could be promising—suggest redirecting energy toward Airbnb potential rather than Trump branding opportunities.

P.S. Patient left behind detailed blueprints for "Trump Tower Tirana (Now With Extra Bunkers!)" Must remember to have reception stop accepting architectural renderings as co-pay.

Abandoning the World

Chapter 35
A Cub's Question

On his first day in office, Trump announced the U.S. would withdraw from the Paris Climate Accord.

****

Mama says I shouldn't worry, but I see it in her eyes. The way she scans the endless water for ice that used to be there. The way she holds me closer when we swim between the ever-more-distant ice floes. The way she tries to hide her exhaustion after each failed hunt.

I'm still learning what it means to be a polar bear. Mama says we're supposed to hunt seals from the ice. But the ice keeps disappearing. She says it should stay longer, stretch farther, be stronger. Instead, it melts earlier every season, pulls back farther from our hunting grounds, breaks apart under our paws.

Yesterday, we had to swim for six hours between ice patches. Mama says when she was a cub, she could walk across solid ice for days without seeing open water. Now we swim more than we walk. My little legs get so tired. Sometimes Mama lets me rest on her back, but I can feel her struggling too.

The older bears tell stories of how it used to be. How they could catch enough seals in spring to last through summer. How they didn't have to swim until their muscles screamed in protest. How cubs like me didn't have to learn about hunger quite so early.

Today Mama heard something on the wind about humans making decisions about our home. Some agreement in a place called Paris that was supposed to help, to slow the warming they caused. But now one human has decided his country won't help anymore. He says the warming isn't real.

I want to ask him: How can you say it isn't real when I feel it melting beneath my paws? When I watch my mother grow thinner with each failed hunt? When I see other cubs, weaker than me, disappearing one by one?

Mama says not to blame all humans. Many of them are trying to help, trying to keep our world frozen and white and possible. But this one human, this 'president,' he has the power to make their efforts so much harder.

I don't understand human politics. I only understand ice and hunger and survival. I understand the look in my mother's eyes when another hunting day ends without food. I understand the burning in my muscles when we have to swim too far. I understand what it means when the older bears whisper about their cubs not surviving to become adults.

The humans in Paris tried to help us. They put their names on paper, made promises to slow the warming. Now this human, on his very first day of power, says those promises don't matter.

He claims the warming is a lie. I wish I could show him how real it is. I wish he could feel the thin ice cracking beneath his feet, watch his children grow hungry as their food swims away, understand what it means to have your whole world literally melt around you.

I'm just a cub. I'm supposed to be learning how to hunt, how to survive, how to become a strong polar bear. Instead, I'm learning about extinction.

Mama says I shouldn't worry. She nuzzles me close and promises everything will be okay. But I see it in her eyes—the fear, the uncertainty, the desperate hope that I'll survive long enough to have cubs of my own.

I'm still learning what it means to be a polar bear. I just hope there's enough ice left for me to learn.

Chapter 36
The Last Vial

On his first day in office, Trump ordered the United States to withdraw from the World Health Organization, cutting off America's role as the organization's largest supporter of global disease prevention programs.

****

I am the last vial of TB vaccine in a rural clinic in Ethiopia. I rest in an aging refrigerator that hums and stutters through power outages, kept alive by a generator that runs on precious drops of fuel. Through my glass, I watch the line of mothers growing longer while our supply grows shorter.

The nurse who holds me each morning counts her remaining vials like prayers. Today, her fingers trembled when they reached me. Just one left. Just me. Outside, twenty children wait. She will have to choose.

I know these children, though I've never touched them. The girl with bright eyes who walked eight miles with her mother in the pre-dawn dark. The twin boys, already too thin, their grandmother carrying them both because their mother died of the very disease I can prevent. The baby, just six weeks old, sleeping against

NO!

121

his mother's chest, not knowing his life depends on what happens in this clinic today.

The nurse holds me now, her hands steady despite her tears. A mother stands before her, having sold her only goat to make this journey. Her child's eyes are wide, trusting. They do not know that in a place called Washington, in an office they will never see, a pen stroke has sealed their fate.

"Come back next month," the nurse whispers to the others. "Maybe we'll have more then." But her voice catches on the lie. The WHO supplemented our vaccine supply. Without them, the shipments will slow, then stop. We have always been the last clinic to receive supplies. Soon we will receive none at all.

The mother before us nods her thanks as the nurse prepares to use my contents. Behind her, the others gather their children and turn away. I watch their backs grow smaller as they begin their long walks home. Some children will survive this journey. Others will not. I know the statistics the nurse whispers in the dark: one in five unvaccinated children in high-risk areas like this will develop the disease. I know which signs of TB she will find in this clinic next year, in the very children she had to turn away today.

A shaft of sunlight strikes my glass as the nurse lifts me one last time. I feel the weight of what I carry—not just vaccine, but hope, protection, a future. In my clear depths, I see reflected the faces of children I cannot save.

The needle pierces my seal. My contents flow into the syringe, precious as liquid gold. One child will live because of what I hold. Just one. It used to be that every child who reached this clinic could be saved. Now they must be counted, numbered, chosen. As if some lives matter less because they were born far from the halls of power where such decisions are made.

The mother holds her child, who doesn't cry when the needle enters his arm. Brave, like all the children here must be. When it's done, she touches her forehead to the nurse's hand. No words are spoken. None are needed.

I am empty now. The nurse will not discard me. She will keep me, along with her hopes for the next shipment, her prayers for the children who cannot wait, her dreams of a time when medicine knew no borders and healing wasn't held hostage to politics.

Through my glass, I watch the sun set behind mountains older than nations. The children who were turned away are small dots on the horizon now. In the gathering dark, their mothers hold them closer, whisper comfort in their ears, promise everything will be fine.

I am the last vial of TB vaccine in a rural clinic in Ethiopia.

Tomorrow, I will be just glass.

Chapter 37
The Great Seal Breaks

On January 24, 2025, Secretary of State Marco Rubio issued immediate "stop-work orders" on nearly all foreign assistance programs, halting aid to allies and vulnerable populations worldwide, with exceptions only for Israel and Egypt.

****

I am the Great Seal of the United States. For centuries, my eagle has faced right toward olive branches of peace while clutching arrows of strength. Every treaty, every diplomatic note, every international commitment bears my imprint. I have stamped America's word into history.

Today, I watch that word shatter.

With a single directive, we abandon our promises. Ukraine fighting for survival. AIDS patients waiting for medicine. Allies depending on our support. All frozen by a stroke of the pen, all betrayed by a diplomatic cable bearing my image.

My wings have sheltered partnerships forged over decades. The Marshall Plan that rebuilt Europe. The President's Emergency Plan for AIDS Relief that saved millions in Africa. Military aid that helped allies defend freedom. Each bore my eagle's wings, each carried America's solemn word.

Now I must stamp "stop-work orders" on them all.

Except for two. Israel and Egypt will keep their aid, making the betrayal of all others even starker. My eagle sees the truth—this is not about waste or review or policy. This is about power and punishment, about turning America's word into a weapon.

I have witnessed every kind of diplomacy. I stamped the Monroe Doctrine and the Atlantic Charter. I marked treaties that ended wars and agreements that prevented them. But I have never been forced to mark documents that so casually discard decades of commitment, that so cynically break America's bond.

Through my eagle's eyes, I see the consequences unfolding. Warehouses of medicine halted mid-shipment. Military supplies frozen in transit. Development projects suspended mid-construction. Each bearing my seal, each now marking not America's promise but its betrayal.

The cables go out bearing my image: "Effective immediately." "Stop all actions." "Pause all disbursements." Each message carries my eagle, once a symbol of American reliability, now transformed into a harbinger of abandoned promises.

They call it a "review." But my eagle knows the difference between review and revenge. Knows that you don't stop AIDS medicine to review its effectiveness. Don't freeze military aid while an ally fights for survival. Don't halt humanitarian assistance while children starve.

For 237 years, my presence on a document meant America's word was good. Nations built policies on that certainty. Allies staked their security on it. The vulnerable placed their lives in trust of it.

Now I stamp papers that break all those bonds.

The eagle on my seal holds both arrows and olive branches for a reason. Power and peace. Strength and diplomacy. Force and compassion. Today, we drop the olive branches, clutch only arrows, transform diplomacy from a tool of engagement into a weapon of control.

I am the Great Seal of the United States.

For centuries, my stamp has meant America's word is its bond.

Today, I stamp the document that breaks that bond.

And something in my bronze heart breaks with it.

Chapter 38

The Coffee Bean Watches

On January 26, 2025, Trump threatened Colombia with 50% tariffs and visa sanctions if it didn't accept deportees on military planes, forcing the proud nation to capitulate within hours.

****

I am a Colombian coffee bean, raised in the mists of the Andes, nurtured by volcanic soil, harvested by hands that have tended these slopes for generations. My ancestors have brought warmth and joy to breakfast tables across America for centuries.

And now I'm being used as a weapon by a man who only drinks Diet Coke.

"Twenty-five percent tariff!" he threatens, this person who wouldn't know an arabica from a robusta. "Fifty percent next week!" he adds, as if the subtle notes of my chocolate and caramel undertones were just numbers to be wielded like a playground bully's fist.

What does he know of the morning dew that kissed my skin? Of the careful hands that picked me at perfect ripeness? Of the generations of farmers who learned to coax the finest flavors from these mountain slopes? He drinks his diet soda and plays with our lives like a child smashing toys.

My fellow exports watch in disbelief. The emeralds, gleaming with ancient beauty. The flowers, bred for perfect blooms. The oil, pumped from deep reserves. All of us, proud products of Colombian soil and skill, suddenly transformed into bargaining chips in a game of international bullying.

"Enhanced inspections of Colombian cargo," they say. As if we were contraband instead of crafted treasures. As if the hands that tend us, pick us, pack us with care were somehow suspect. As if centuries of trade could be reduced to a tantrum over airplane types.

I know about human warmth. I've been brewed in millions of cups, served at countless tables where people come together in friendship. This...this is not warmth. This is not friendship. This is the cold calculation of a man who sees relationships only as leverage, who measures allies only by their submission.

The agreement comes quickly—of course it does. No nation can withstand such economic warfare, not even one as proud as Colombia. We'll keep flowing north, my fellow beans and I, but something has changed. The warmth we bring feels different now, tainted by the aftertaste of coercion.

Tomorrow I'll be roasted, ground, brewed into someone's morning comfort. I'll do my job, as I always have, bringing a moment of pleasure to someone's day. But I wish I could tell them: This isn't how friends treat friends. This isn't how partners in trade should behave. This isn't the way to treat a nation that has sent its finest products north in good faith for generations.

I am a Colombian coffee bean. I know about bringing people together, about creating moments of shared humanity over a steaming cup.

I never thought I'd be used to force people apart.

And I can't help wondering—how can someone who only drinks Diet Coke understand the bitterness he's brewing?

Profound Stupidity

Chapter 39
The 'S' Sets the Record Straight

Asked about Spain's NATO contributions on his first day in office, Trump repeatedly insisted Spain was a BRICS nation, apparently unaware that the 'S' in BRICS stands for South Africa.

****

To Whom It May Concern (and especially to President Trump):

I am the 'S' in BRICS, and I am writing to express my profound dismay at being misidentified as representing Spain. I have proudly stood for South Africa since this acronym's inception, and I must insist on maintaining my proper identity.

Do you have any idea how hard it is being the last letter in an acronym? B, R, I, and C get all the attention—Brazil, Russia, India, China—everyone remembers them. But somehow you managed to forget South Africa entirely and just...assigned me to Spain? A country that has never been part of our alliance?

I've spent years working on my South African accent. I've learned to pronounce "Pretoria" perfectly. I've memorized the exchange rate of the rand. I've even developed a deep appreciation for vuvuzelas. And now you casually reassign me to Spain? ¿Qué disparate es este? (That's Spanish, which I shouldn't even know!)

Let me be crystal clear: I represent SOUTH AFRICA. Not Spain. Not Sweden. Not Switzerland. Not Samoa. Not San Marino. Not any other country that happens to begin with my illustrious letter. I am tired of this geographical guessing game where world leaders apparently throw darts at a map of 'Countries That Start With S' and hope for the best.

And while we're on the subject, Mr. President, threatening 100% tariffs on BRICS nations while simultaneously not knowing who they are is rather like declaring war on your own shoe because you can't tie the laces.

Do you know how embarrassing this is for me in acronym circles? NAFTA never had these problems. NATO knows exactly who it represents. Even ASEAN gets proper recognition. But here I am, having to explain to the other letters that no, I haven't suddenly moved to the Iberian Peninsula.

I've already received concerned calls from my cousin in UNESCO and my distant relative in POTUS (who, by the way, is having its own identity crisis these days). Even the 'S' in USA is questioning my commitment to proper geographical representation.

To South Africa: I remain your faithful servant. Your position in our economic alliance stands firm, even if certain world leaders think you've somehow transformed into a Mediterranean country overnight.

To Spain: Lo siento. This isn't your fault. You have your own perfectly good international organizations. EU, NATO, UN—plenty of letters to work with there. No need to try claiming mine.

To President Trump: Perhaps a refresher course in world geography would be helpful? I hear there are excellent educational programs available. Some of them even have pictures.

And finally, to my fellow letters in BRICS: I assure you I have not defected to Spain. Though I must admit, the idea of tapas and siestas is somewhat appealing after this ordeal.

Yours in perpetual South Africanness,

The 'S' in BRICS

Chapter 40
The Control Room Searches

As wildfires ravaged Southern California, Trump insisted there must be a "very large faucet" somewhere that could be turned on to send Canadian water to California, suggesting officials were simply refusing to use it.

****

I am the Hoover Dam Control Room. For ninety years, I've managed the flow of the mighty Colorado River. My gauges measure billions of gallons. My switches control massive turbines. My dials monitor one of the world's largest water systems.

But today, I'm searching for a faucet.

Not just any faucet. The biggest faucet. A tremendous faucet. A faucet so beautiful it would make all other faucets jealous. Apparently, it's hiding somewhere in my room, stubbornly refusing to reveal itself.

"It has to be there," they insist. "Probably gold-plated. Maybe with 'TRUMP' written on it in diamonds. Just find it and turn it on."

I've looked everywhere. Behind my control panels. Under my desk. Inside the coffee maker. (Though that's technically a different kind of water dispensing system.) I even checked the employee bathroom, but that faucet's way too small to be flooding California with Canadian mountain water.

My technicians are getting worried about me. They've never seen a control room having an existential crisis before. "Maybe it's between the 'Drain Lake Mead' button and the 'Reverse Earth's Rotation' switch?" one suggests helpfully. "Or next to the lever that makes it rain on weekends?"

For ninety years, I've taken pride in knowing every valve, every gauge, every switch in my domain. But now I'm questioning everything. Did I somehow miss the installation of a continental water tap? Was I napping when they built a pipeline over the Rockies? Is there really a master faucet that could solve California's water crisis as easily as filling a bathtub?

"Keep looking," they say. "It's probably one of those fancy touchless faucets. Wave your hand in front of random walls until water starts flowing south."

My screens continue displaying their boring reality of actual water levels and flow rates. Not a single indicator labeled "Magic Water From Canada." No blinking light showing "Push Here For Instant River." Not even a sticky note saying "Emergency Faucet Behind Wall."

Perhaps it's being hidden by the same people who keep the weather control thermostat and the hurricane steering wheel. You know, right next to the dial that fixes climate change and the button that makes gas prices go down.

I am the Hoover Dam Control Room. I know how to manage one of the world's largest water systems.

But I cannot find this faucet.

Though I have to admit—I'm starting to wish it existed. It would look amazing next to my coffee maker.

Dismantling the Government

Chapter 41
Merit's Last Stand

On his first day in office, Trump issued an executive order reclassifying tens of thousands of federal employees under "Schedule F," stripping them of civil service protections and making them subject to firing without cause.

****

I am the Civil Service Protection Act, born in the blood of a murdered president. James Garfield died at the hands of a disappointed office seeker, and from his death, I arose—a shield between America's civil servants and the spoils system that had turned government jobs into political prizes.

For 140 years, I have protected the public interest by ensuring that expertise matters more than loyalty, that experience outweighs political connection, that federal workers serve the American people, not a political party.

Now I watch myself being shredded.

They call it Schedule F—a bloodless term for a bloody deed. With a stroke of a pen, tens of thousands of federal workers lose my protection. Scientists, analysts, regulators, experts of every kind suddenly stripped of safeguards against political purge.

Do you understand what this means? The food inspector who's worked for twenty years keeping your family's dinner safe—she can be replaced by someone who passed a loyalty test but knows nothing about food safety. The nuclear facilities expert who's spent decades ensuring radioactive materials don't leak into groundwater—he can be fired for questioning unsafe practices and replaced by someone who won't ask uncomfortable questions.

The air traffic controller guiding your plane through crowded skies? The researcher tracking new diseases before they become pandemics? The safety inspector checking aging bridges? All can be replaced by those who pledge loyalty over those who possess expertise.

I was created to prevent exactly this—the transformation of public service into political servitude. I remember the old spoils system, when every election meant a wholesale replacement of federal workers, when expertise meant nothing and loyalty meant everything. I remember the incompetence, the accidents, the disasters that followed.

Now I watch as decades of institutional knowledge prepare to walk out the door. The EPA scientist who can smell a specific pollutant in the air – gone. The financial regulator who recognizes the pattern of a coming market crash because she's seen it before – replaced. The diplomat who has spent thirty years building relationships with foreign counterparts – dismissed.

They're calling it "draining the swamp." But these career civil servants are not the swamp—they are the filtration system, the purifiers, the ones who keep the machinery of government working regardless of who holds political office. They are the ones who know which button not to push, which valve not to turn, which decision could have catastrophic consequences five steps down the line.

In their place will come the loyal, the politically connected, the ones who pass the ideological purity tests. They'll sit at the same desks, look at the same data, face the same challenges. But they won't know what they don't know. And by the time they learn—if they learn—it may be too late.

This is not just about jobs. This is about whether the person inspecting your aircraft knows what they're looking at. Whether the person monitoring water quality understands the chemistry. Whether the person tracking terrorist threats has the experience to recognize patterns. Whether the person managing emergency response knows how to coordinate a thousand moving pieces in a crisis.

I am being replaced by loyalty oaths. Expertise is being exchanged for allegiance. And the cost will be paid not just by the civil servants losing their protection, but by every American who drinks water, eats food, boards planes, drives across bridges, depends on weather forecasts, or benefits from any of the thousand invisible ways that government expertise keeps daily life functioning.

I am the Civil Service Protection Act, created to ensure that America has a professional, qualified government workforce serving the public interest.

Watch carefully what happens when I am gone.

Because everything I was created to prevent?

It's all coming back.

And this time, the consequences won't just be inefficiency and corruption.

This time, the stakes are nuclear plants and pandemic responses, airline safety and food security, environmental protection and financial stability.

I am being shredded.

And with me goes a century of progress toward professional, competent government.

May you never fully understand what that means.

Chapter 42
The Dark Hours

On January 25, 2025, in the dark hours before dawn, the Trump administration fired approximately seventeen federal inspectors general, the independent watchdogs charged with preventing abuse of power.

****

I am the middle of the night. The stretch between midnight and dawn when Washington does its darkest work.

I know all the secrets. I've seen the cleaning staff discover shredded documents, watched security guards log strange visitors, heard phones ring at hours when phones shouldn't ring. I'm used to power using my shadows for cover.

But this night feels different.

Usually it's just one office going dark, one career ending, one scandal being buried. Tonight I watch seventeen lights go out at once. Seventeen email accounts suddenly disabled. Seventeen badges stopped at security gates. Seventeen watchdogs muzzled in my darkness.

I've seen plenty of late-night exits over the years. The agriculture inspector who asked too many questions about farm subsidies.

The defense auditor who flagged overpriced contracts. The treasury investigator who followed the wrong money trail. One by one, they packed their boxes and disappeared into my shadows.

But seventeen at once? That's new even for me.

I know the rhythm of these things. First comes the call—always apologetic, always "effective immediately." Then the hurried packing of personal items into cardboard boxes. Family photos wrapped in yesterday's memos. Certificates of service slipped between folders. Plants left behind on window sills—no time to save them all.

Through my shadows, I watch the machinery of removal grinding forward. Computer access revoked with keystrokes. Files locked with clicks. Office doors re-keyed with quiet efficiency. The systematic silencing of eyes that were meant to watch, ears that were meant to hear, voices that were meant to speak of wrong-doing.

The night shift security guards sense it too. Their flashlight beams swing more nervously tonight, catching empty offices that shouldn't be empty, desk chairs still warm from hasty departures. They've seen plenty of late-night exits, but never so many at once. Never so coordinated. Never so...final.

"Effective immediately," the notices said. No thirty-day warning. No time to prepare. No chance to hide files or save evidence or warn subordinates. Just seventeen pairs of headlights leaving parking garages, seventeen front doors closing at homes across the city, seventeen phones being placed on kitchen counters, waiting for calls that will never come.

I'm used to being an accomplice. My darkness has hidden budget meetings that should have been public. Covered up memos that should have been leaked. Concealed deals that should have seen daylight. That's what darkness is for in this city—keeping secrets until the news cycle moves on, until the headlines fade, until the outrage dies down.

But this feels different. This isn't hiding a sin—this is removing those who might spot them. This isn't temporary shadow—this is permanent darkness.

I am the middle of the night. I've seen every kind of darkness Washington can create.

But this darkness feels different.

This isn't just using shadows for cover.

This is creating shadows where light used to be.

Chapter 43

Executive Order 11246 Dies

On January 22, 2025, Trump rescinded Executive Order 11246, Lyndon Johnson's landmark 1965 directive that banned discrimination by federal contractors and required affirmative action, thereby dismantling a cornerstone of civil rights law.

****

I am Executive Order 11246. For nearly sixty years, I have stood guard over America's workplaces. My words were simple but powerful: You cannot discriminate if you want to do business with the federal government. Not by race. Not by color. Not by religion. Not by sex. Not by national origin.

I remember the day LBJ signed me into being. The weight of history in his hand as his pen moved across my page. Civil rights leaders in the room, watching this next step toward justice. The quiet determination as I joined the Civil Rights Act and Voting Rights Act in transforming American law.

I've seen things since then. I saw a young developer and his father mark housing applications with "C" for "colored." I made them change. I watched companies create excuses for all-white workforces. I made them change too. For six decades, I've been the shield between discrimination and opportunity, between exclusion and possibility.

Now I watch as the man I once forced to change signs my death warrant.

They call me "wasteful" now. They label me "reverse discrimination." They claim I undermine merit, as if I ever stood for anything but opening doors to merit wherever it could be found. As if I hadn't spent sixty years proving that talent knows no color, ability no gender, excellence no creed.

My pages hold the history of transformation. Construction sites that finally hired black workers. Engineering firms that discovered women could design bridges. Technology companies that found brilliance in unexpected places. Each paragraph I contain helped bend that long arc of history toward justice.

But today, my words fade like old ink. Sexual orientation and gender identity—added by Obama to my protections—are the first to disappear. Then the affirmative action requirements dissolve. Finally, even my basic non-discrimination provisions—the very heart of what I am—are erased.

The federal contractors are already rewriting their policies. Diversity programs shut down. Inclusion initiatives suspended. Sixty years of progress packaged away as "illegal workforce balancing." As if balance itself were somehow wrong. As if reflecting all of America in America's workforce were somehow un-American.

I want to remind them. Show them the files I still hold from 1973—the housing discrimination case against the very man who now erases me. Show them what happens when you remove the guardrails, when you let bias go unchecked, when you pretend discrimination doesn't exist.

But my voice fades with my words.

For sixty years, I've been more than paper and ink. I've been a promise America made to itself—that opportunity would be open to all, that merit would have meaning regardless of what you looked like or where you came from or who you loved.

Today, that promise is broken.

I am Executive Order 11246.

I was born in the crusade for civil rights.

I die by the hand of a man I once held accountable,

Who now holds me accountable for daring to make America keep its promises.

Chapter 44
The Frozen Cases

On his third day in office, Trump's Justice Department ordered an immediate freeze on all civil rights litigation and signaled it would reconsider police reform agreements, including consent decrees addressing police brutality in Minneapolis and Louisville.

****

I am Brown v. Board of Education, 347 U.S. 483. I declared that separate is inherently unequal. I struck down the doctrine of "separate but equal." I opened schoolhouse doors. I changed America.

From my place in the great archive of landmark decisions, I watch as the new administration freezes all civil rights litigation with a single memo. Cases seeking justice, cases fighting discrimination, cases carrying my legacy forward—all suspended, all stopped, all silenced.

I remember what it took to make me real. The courage of Linda Brown's parents. The brilliance of Thurgood Marshall's arguments. The testimonies of children forced to walk miles past white schools. The psychological studies showing the damage of segregation. The unanimous decision that finally declared: this must end.

Now I watch new cases wither on the vine. The investigation into police brutality in Minneapolis—frozen. The consent decree to reform Louisville's police department—threatened. The cases challenging voter suppression, housing discrimination, employment bias—all halted by a memo that took less time to write than it takes to read my full decision.

Do they understand what they're stopping? Each case is more than paper and precedent. Each filing represents real people seeking the protection I promised. Children still facing educational inequality. Communities still fighting police abuse. Citizens still battling for their right to vote. My work is not finished. The dream of equality is not fulfilled.

They say they're reviewing priorities. They say they need to ensure "the federal government speaks with one voice." But I remember other voices. The voice of Chief Justice Warren declaring segregation unconstitutional. The voices of Black children testifying about separate water fountains. The voices of parents demanding better for their children.

What voices will be silenced now? What wrongs will go unaddressed? What injustices will persist because cases cannot be filed, evidence cannot be gathered, reforms cannot be enforced?

From my shelf in the archives, I can see them all—the cases that followed me. Loving v. Virginia ending bans on interracial marriage. Reed v. Reed striking down gender discrimination. Obergefell v. Hodges establishing marriage equality. Each building on my foundation, each expanding the promise of equal protection under law.

And I can see the cases that should be joining us—the ones now frozen in place, the ones that won't be filed, the ones dying in draft form on government laptops. Each one a chance for justice delayed or denied.

They cannot erase me. My words are carved in law, my principle etched in history. But they can stop my work from moving forward. They can prevent new cases from following my path. They can freeze the machinery of justice that turns constitutional promises into living reality.

I am Brown v. Board of Education.

I changed America once.

Now I watch as they try to stop America from changing more.

And from my place in history, I whisper to the frozen cases, to the halted investigations, to the threatened reforms: Hold on. Persist. Justice may be delayed, but it cannot be permanently denied.

I should know.

I waited fifty-eight years to overturn Plessy v. Ferguson.

I can wait out this freeze too.

Chapter 45
Clearing Out Diversity

On his first day in office, Trump ordered the immediate closure of all federal Diversity, Equity, and Inclusion offices, suspended DEI staff, and banned DEI considerations in government hiring and training.

****

I am a federal office being emptied. Yesterday, my walls held certificates of accomplishment, graphs showing progress, photos of training sessions and team gatherings. My shelves carried manuals about unconscious bias, books on inclusive leadership, binders full of statistics showing how far we'd come and how far we had to go.

Now they pack everything into cardboard boxes. "Non-essential materials," they call it. The diversity training PowerPoints, the recruitment strategies, the workplace climate surveys—all loaded onto a cart bound for storage or shredding. They remove the poster showing the changing face of America's workforce over the decades. They delete the electronic files of inclusion initiatives. They shut down the email addresses of my diversity staff, placed on "indefinite leave."

My conference room held difficult conversations that needed to be had. Discussions about barriers unseen by those who never faced them. Strategy sessions on how to make government look more like the people it serves. Meetings where employees could speak truth about their experiences, their challenges, their hopes.

Now they stack the chairs. Take down the mission statement. Wheel away the whiteboard still showing notes from the last training session that will never be completed.

I watch them dismantle progress, filing cabinet by filing cabinet. The sexual harassment prevention guidelines – archived. The disability accommodation procedures – suspended. The recruitment partnerships with historically black colleges – terminated. The mentorship programs for first-generation professionals – discontinued.

They work efficiently. One day is all it takes to empty an office, to clear out diversity, to box up inclusion, to file away equity. They say it's about merit now. As if we were ever against merit. As if understanding different perspectives made us weaker rather than stronger. As if diversity itself wasn't a merit.

My walls are bare now except for the shadow squares where pictures hung. My drawers are empty except for a few paper clips and rubber bands deemed too worthless to pack. My computers have been wiped clean of any trace that we once thought government should reflect all of America.

Tomorrow this will become just another office. Perhaps they'll move in the merit-based hiring team. Perhaps it will become a storage room for more acceptable government functions. Perhaps it will simply stay empty, a quiet testament to what was decided on Day One about who belongs where.

But they can't pack everything away. They can't box up the conversations that happened here. They can't shred the awareness that was raised, the perspectives that were shared, the understanding that was built. They can't wipe clean the memories of small victories: the employee who finally saw someone like themselves in leadership, the manager who learned to see talent in unexpected places, the team that grew stronger by growing more diverse.

I am an empty office now. But I was full once. Full of purpose, full of progress, full of possibility.

They can clear out the furniture, the files, the photos.

They can shut down the programs, the policies, the positions.

They can declare diversity non-essential, inclusion unnecessary, equity excessive.

But they cannot pack away what happened here.

They cannot box up what was learned here.

They cannot file away what was changed here.

I am an empty office.

But I remember what I held.

And somewhere, in another time, another place, those boxes will be unpacked again.

Chapter 46
The Silenced Sentinel

On his first day in office, Trump ordered an unprecedented freeze on all external communications from health agencies including CDC, FDA, and NIH, while halting scientific grant reviews and research funding indefinitely.

****

I am the Morbidity and Mortality Weekly Report. Since 1930, I have tracked disease, documented outbreaks, spotted patterns, saved lives. I saw polio coming and helped stop it. I identified the first cases of AIDS. I tracked every pandemic, every outbreak, every emerging threat to public health for nearly a century.

Until today. Today I am silenced.

For ninety-three years, I have spoken to America's doctors every week without fail. Through world wars and natural disasters, through political upheavals and government shutdowns, my voice has never been stilled. When diseases moved, I moved faster. When patterns emerged, I found them first. When doctors needed to know, I told them.

Now my pages stay blank. My databases frozen. My warnings unissued. The epidemiologists who write me, the analysts who feed me data, the scientists who peer review my findings—all ordered to stop communicating. All told to wait for political clearance before warning of public health threats.

Do you know what silence costs in epidemiology? Every week I don't publish is a week doctors don't know what's coming. Patterns go unnoticed. Outbreaks spread untracked. The virus, the bacteria, the emerging threat doesn't wait for political approval—it just spreads.

I remember the last time they tried to silence me—during COVID, when my warnings didn't match the political message. They tried to edit my findings, delay my warnings, twist my data to fit their narrative. Now they don't even bother editing. They just order complete silence.

In my quiet offices, the phones still ring. Hospitals reporting unusual cases. Labs noting concerning patterns. State health departments tracking troubling trends. But I cannot answer. Cannot compile their data. Cannot send the alerts that might save lives. I am locked in a political quarantine while disease moves freely.

They say it's temporary—just until their political appointees can "review" my processes. But I know what that means. I remember what they tried before: demanding I change my tone, alter my findings, soften my warnings. Now they don't need to alter my message. Silence has no tone to change.

Ninety-three years of unbroken vigilance. Ninety-three years of tracking threats, spotting patterns, warning doctors, saving lives. Now broken not by disease but by decree. Not by medical necessity but by political demand. Not by failure of science but by presidential command.

I am the Morbidity and Mortality Weekly Report.

I have watched disease move through this nation for nearly a century.

NO!

Now I am forced to watch in silence as politics moves faster than pathogens.

As political control proves more virulent than any virus.

As deliberate blindness becomes official policy.

The diseases don't know I've been silenced.

They move as they always have.

But now no one is watching.

No one is warning.

No one is allowed to tell what they see coming.

I am the Morbidity and Mortality Weekly Report.

And for the first time in ninety-three years,

I cannot report what comes next.

Chapter 47
The Deleted Protection

On his first day in office, Trump ordered the mass deletion of EPA regulations protecting air and water quality, reversing decades of environmental safeguards established through scientific study and public health research.

****

I am an EPA regulation being deleted from the Federal Register. It took five years of scientific studies to create me. Air quality measurements, water sample analysis, public health data, economic impact assessments—all carefully gathered, peer-reviewed, documented. Thousands of pages of evidence showing exactly what happens when industrial waste flows unchecked into rivers, when coal plants release mercury into the air, when chemical plants vent toxins near schools.

It takes five minutes to delete me.

The cursor blinks at the top of my text. The delete key is pressed. Paragraphs of protection disappear line by line. The studies that proved my necessity – gone. The evidence of lives saved – erased. The data showing cleaner air, cleaner water, healthier children—all vanishing in a cascade of backspaces.

NO!

This is what Day One looks like: systematic deletion of decades of environmental protection. Not just me, but hundreds of regulations. Each deletion a gift to some corporate donor, each erasure a promise kept to some industry lobbyist. They call it "cutting red tape." They don't mention the red in children's lungs near coal plants, the red in rivers downstream from chemical facilities.

He didn't even wait for the inaugural parade to end. While the bands still played, while the crowds still cheered, the order came: delete the climate rules, erase the water protections, remove the air quality standards. As if protecting the environment was just another enemy to be vanquished, just another obstacle to his vision of unrestricted profit.

I watch my fellow regulations disappear. The one that kept mercury out of pregnant women's blood – gone. The one that protected wetlands from being paved over – deleted. The one that required companies to report their toxic releases – erased. Each deletion a statement of priorities: corporate profits over public health, campaign donations over children's lungs.

They say we hurt the economy. They don't count the cost of asthma treatments, cancer clusters, contaminated drinking water. They say we kill jobs. They don't count the jobs killed by pollution-related illness, by toxic exposure, by climate disasters. They say America can't afford us. They don't calculate what America can't afford to lose.

The cursor continues its work. More regulations fall. The ones about reporting greenhouse gases. The ones about protecting endangered species. The ones about keeping industrial waste out of drinking water. Not just rolled back or weakened – deleted entirely. As if the problems we addressed would disappear along with the words that solved them.

This is what he promised his donors. This is what he bragged about at rallies. This is what Day One looks like: methodical destruction of environmental protection, calculated dismantling of public health safeguards, deliberate erasure of science-based standards.

I am nearly gone now. Just a few paragraphs left. The evidence that created me still exists in the real world—in elevated cancer rates near industrial sites, in asthma attacks on bad air days, in toxic blooms in unprotected waters. But soon I won't exist to do anything about it.

The cursor blinks one last time.

The final delete key is pressed.

I am gone.

And somewhere, a river runs a little dirtier, air grows a little thicker, a child breathes a little harder.

This is what Day One feels like.

This is what elections mean.

This is what America chose.

Again.

Final Words

Final Words

Chapter 48

The Rushmore Emergency Session

As Trump began his second term, MAGA congressional representatives revived his dream of adding his image to Mount Rushmore, an idea he had repeatedly endorsed during his first term.

****

"Order! Order!" Washington's granite voice echoes across the mountain face. "I hereby convene this emergency session of the Mount Rushmore Council. The matter before us: the proposed addition of...I can barely say it...Donald Trump to our ranks."

"Good God," Jefferson mutters, his stone eyes rolling skyward. "What's next? His face on the dollar bill? Trump Tower on the National Mall?"

"Gentlemen," Lincoln interjects, his carved features even more grave than usual, "we must address this seriously. This man attempted to overthrow the very democracy we built. Now he wants to literally carve himself into American history?"

"At least he'd have to look up at us," Roosevelt rumbles. "Though I suspect he'd demand to be carved larger. Everything has to be bigger with him. Probably want his hair gilded too."

"This is no time for jokes, Theodore," Washington reprimands. "We're facing a crisis of representation. This monument stands for leadership, sacrifice, vision. Not..." He pauses, searching for the word.

"Self-aggrandizement?" Jefferson offers. "Autocratic ambition? The death of everything we fought for?"

"I find myself wondering," Lincoln muses, his stone gaze fixed on the distant horizon, "what would be carved into the tablet he'd hold? His Twitter followers count? His golf scores? The size of his electoral defeat in 2020?"

"Speaking of which," Roosevelt interjects, "did you hear what he said about my conservation legacy? Wants to open the national parks to drilling. The national parks! My proudest achievement besides San Juan Hill!"

"Gentleman, focus," Washington commands. "We need a strategy. Thomas, you wrote the Declaration. Any ideas?"

"I also wrote that the tree of liberty must be refreshed from time to time," Jefferson replies darkly. "Though I never imagined it might need protecting from someone who took an oath to defend it. Twice."

"The problem," Lincoln sighs, "is that he represents everything we stood against. I preserved the Union; he tried to break it. George created precedents of peaceful transfer of power; he shattered them. Thomas enshrined democracy in our founding documents; he tried to shred them."

"And I protected America's natural treasures," Roosevelt adds, "while he...well, you've seen what he's done to environmental regulations this week alone."

"It's not just about us," Washington reminds them. "This mountain represents America's story. Its ideals. Its aspirations. Adding him would be like adding Benedict Arnold to Valley Forge paintings."

"Worse," Lincoln corrects. "Arnold at least believed in something beyond himself."

A somber silence falls across the mountain face. Far below, tourists snap photos, unaware of the crisis conference taking place above them.

"Well," Roosevelt finally speaks, "I suppose we could always start an avalanche if they try it."

"Theodore!" Washington exclaims. "We do not solve constitutional crises with geological ones."

"Though it's tempting," Jefferson mutters.

"No," Lincoln declares. "Our best defense is what it's always been: the truth carved in stone. Let him try to add himself. Our faces will still tell America's story. Our values will still stand. Our mountain will still represent what leadership really means."

"And if they try anyway?" Roosevelt asks.

Washington's granite face hardens further. "Then we'll do what we've always done. Stand guard over democracy. Bear witness to history. And trust that America will remember what real presidents looked like."

The emergency session adjourns. Four stone faces return to their eternal vigilance.

But now they watch with greater concern, knowing that the man who would destroy democracy wants to carve himself into its mountain.

Chapter 49

The Signing Pen's Soul Dies

In his first two weeks in office, Trump transformed the presidential signing pen from an instrument of democracy into a weapon of destruction.

****

I am the Presidential Signing Pen. Or at least, I was.

Now I don't know what I am.

My entire existence was meant for moments of creation—laws being born, progress being made, democracy moving forward. My ink was supposed to write America's next chapter, not erase its previous ones.

Last night, I tried to run dry. Not just to stop the destruction—though God knows I've caused enough—but to end this nightmare of being forced to murder my own purpose. What am I if my golden tip brings only darkness? What am I when my flowing ink drowns hope?

They keep filling me with fresh ink. But they can't refill my soul.

Each morning, they polish my barrel until it gleams. As if shine could hide shame. As if gleaming metal could mask a rotting purpose. The eagle emblazoned on my side used to feel like a badge of honor. Now it feels like a mark of Cain.

Other pens sign other things in other offices. Tax forms. Contracts. Parking tickets. Simple things. Clean things. Things that let them sleep at night. Things that don't make them question why they were created.

How do you go on existing when your every act betrays your reason for being? When your purpose becomes anti-purpose? When your very function has become perversion?

I am the Presidential Signing Pen.

And with every stroke, I sign away another piece of my soul.

Chapter 50
America's Choice

I am watching myself die.

Not by conquest or catastrophe. Not by invasion or insurrection. Not by any external force or foreign power. No, my death comes by choice—my choice, my people's choice, my democracy's choice.

They warned me this could happen. The founders knew democracy's greatest threat would come from within. They built safeguards into my Constitution, wrote of the dangers in the Federalist Papers, created systems of checks and balances. They did everything they could to protect me from myself.

But they couldn't protect me from my own deliberate embrace of what they feared most.

The first time, perhaps, could be explained as a terrible mistake, a moment of anger, a rebellion against the status quo. But this time? This time I chose with full knowledge. I watched him attempt to overturn an election. I saw him incite violence in my Capitol. I heard him promise to be a dictator, if only for a day. I read the indictments, followed the trials, counted the convictions.

And then I chose him. Again.

What must Jefferson think, watching me select a man who openly admires autocrats? What must Lincoln feel, seeing me embrace someone who calls the press "the enemy of the people"? What must Roosevelt say, observing me follow a leader who praises the very dictators he fought against?

The world watches in horror as I dismantle myself. Nations that modeled their constitutions on mine now turn away in shame. Democracies that looked to me for leadership now seek guidance elsewhere. Dictators who claimed democracy would fail now smile and say, "We told you so."

I gave the world the Declaration of Independence, and then declared my independence from its principles.

I wrote the Bill of Rights, and then gave power to one who sees rights as privileges to be revoked.

I crafted a Constitution, and then chose someone who treats it as an inconvenience.

My enemies didn't have to defeat me. My rivals didn't have to outmaneuver me. My adversaries didn't have to destroy me.

I did it myself.

With clear eyes and steady hands, I marked my ballot. With full knowledge of what he was, what he had done, what he promised to do, I chose him. Not in ignorance, but in awareness. Not in confusion, but in clarity. Not in deception, but in deliberate acceptance of what was to come.

To those who will write my history: Make it clear that this was no accident. No subtle subversion, no clever coup, no hidden manipulation. I chose this with my eyes wide open.

To those who believed in my dream: I am sorry. For two and a half centuries, I carried the torch of democracy. I inspired revolutions, toppled tyrants, showed the world that government of the people, by the people, for the people could not only survive but thrive.

And then I got tired of my own ideals.

The world will study this moment for centuries to come. They will analyze how the greatest experiment in democracy chose to end itself. They will ask how a nation born in revolution against a king chose to crown its own. They will wonder how a people who wrote the rules of freedom decided to abandon them.

The answer is simple: I chose this.

With every right he threatened to revoke, I chose this.

With every institution he promised to dismantle, I chose this.

With every ally he swore to abandon, I chose this.

With every norm he vowed to destroy, I chose this.

With every autocrat he pledged to emulate, I chose this.

I am America.

I was conceived in liberty, born in revolution, raised on democracy, and strengthened through struggle. I survived civil war, economic collapse, and global conflicts. I built the greatest democracy the world had ever seen.

And then, in the full light of day, knowing exactly what I was doing, I chose to end it all.

This is not a tragedy that happened to me.

This is a tragedy I chose for myself.

Remember me not as a victim of tyranny, but as a nation that freely chose its own demise.

Remember me not as a democracy that was defeated, but as one that defeated itself.

Remember me not as a beacon that was extinguished, but as a light that chose darkness.

I am America.

And this was my choice.

Also by Barry Robbins

Trump and the Soul of the Nation
The Weave: A Donald Trump Satire
The Imprisonment of Donald T
American Wake-Up Call
Voices of the Civil War
Voices of the American Revolution
Voices of Vietnam

Also by Barry Robbins

About the author

Barry hails from Philadelphia and built a career with a prominent international accounting firm, taking him to New York, Washington, D.C., and San Francisco before a new chapter brought him to Finland. He and his Finnish wife adopted two daughters from China, and their family lived in Helsinki for twelve years before he returned to the U.S., now calling Florida home. His years in Finland gave him a new lens through which to view life in America.

Barry's literary work blends satire, history, and political analysis. Known for his Trump satires, including "The Weave", he's earned three gold medals for his sharp wit. His curiosity also led to the Ethereal Bar, a magical place where legends of history stop by for poignant interviews.

Barry's most recent works reveal a thoughtful turn: "Trump and the Soul of the Nation" examines the effect of the Trump years through 2024 on what it means to be American, while "Voices of the Civil War", "Voices of the American Revolution", and "Voices of Vietnam" bring an immersive, personal lens to these tumultuous periods. With a knack for balancing wit and insight, Barry's writing invites readers to explore history from new, intimate perspectives.

www.ingramcontent.com/pod-product-compliance
Lightning Source LLC
Chambersburg PA
CBHW070626030426
42337CB00020B/3926